Nuno Had a Dream

Wolves' Championship Season 2017-18

Before we look back at a memorable season, we should not forget the man who did not play in a single game yet was not forgotten and whose fighting spirit was an on-going inspiration to the Wolves team.

Carl Ikeme was diagnosed with leukaemia before the season started, but his name was chanted at every home game and he delivered a moving message on the Molineux big screen once the title had been clinched. Just as this book was going to press, the great news came through that Carl was in complete remission. We send him further fond wishes and support in his return to good health.

In his end-of-season message to fans Ikeme said: "Hello everyone, I just wanted to congratulate you all on the fantastic season that we've had. I wish I could be there to celebrate with you all but I'm still getting treated and I'm still in recovery. I want to send massive love to the supporters. I hope you enjoy the day. Have a few drinks on me. See you soon."

For every copy sold of this book, 25p will be donated to the Carl Ikeme Cure Leukaemia Fund.

If you wish to make a further contribution to the fund please donate via:

https://www.justgiving.com/campaigns/charity/cureleukaemia/ikeme

#TeamKeme

Nuno Had a Dream

Wolves' Championship Season 2017-18

Dave Harrison
with photographs by
Sam Bagnall

St David's Press

Cardiff

Published in Wales by St. David's Press, an imprint of

Ashley Drake Publishing Ltd
PO Box 733
Cardiff
CF14 7ZY

www.st-davids-press.wales

First Impression – 2018

ISBN
Paperback: 978-1-902719-740

British Library Cataloguing-in-Publication Data.
A CIP catalogue for this book is available from the British Library.

Typeset by Prepress Plus, India (www.prepressplus.in)

Printed by Akcent Press, Czech Republic

CONTENTS

To John 'Foz' Hendley,
lifelong Wolves fan and former member of the club's media department
who sadly passed away during the season

FOREWORD

On occasions I gave up my place in the directors' box and sat with the supporters to get a fans-eye view of this amazing campaign. At first there were a lot of heads shaking with people asking: "What's goin' on 'ere, then?"

There was a lot of scepticism, initially, about what was happening. I shared the doubts that you cannot buy a team, but have to build one. Wolves managed to turn that argument upside down.

Nuno, with Fosun's backing, put together a side which cost a fair bit of money but also created a real unit, and all in the space of a single season. It was a team capable of winning games and playing marvellous football with flair and discipline combined. Over the years that hasn't always been the

Bully in with 'The Pack'.

Bully looks on, with his old strike partner Andy Mutch.

Wolves way. It has usually been a case of getting the ball up front quickly and building from there. In my day it was often: "Let's give it to Bully and Mutchy and see what happens."

The Nuno way is to keep the ball and build gradually. I sometimes think they are guilty of over-doing it, with 15-20 passes, but then Rúben Neves will thread a pass from 50 yards up to the front men and, 'bang', there's another goal.

Neves is some special player. His quality and pedigree were obvious straight away and it was clear that he was too good for the Championship. At some point it was also inevitable he would be linked with the top clubs. To be fair to the lad, he decided he would give us a year and see what happened. His reward was to reach the Premier League and he played a big part in that. Now I think and hope he will stay with us for many more seasons.

So much has been said about the goal he scored against Derby, and a lot more has been written about it in this book. All I will add to the discussion is that it was a goal which stands comparison with any scored by Cristiano Ronaldo and Gareth Bale.

Down among the fans it was easy to see why they took to this team. It was not just the football. It was a while before they appreciated what the new style meant but pretty soon they were thrilled by what they were seeing. Then, in time, they grew to love the way the players responded and showed their appreciation in return.

Bully with chairman Jeff Shi.

There was not too much concern when we lost a game. Whereas in the past gloom would set in, now there was a feeling that we could bounce back from defeat, which is the sign of a good team. That was obvious after we lost to Aston Villa at their place. It was their big result, yet they didn't build on the win. We used that defeat to dig in and grow even stronger.

I would love to have played in this Wolves team – I reckon I would have got 40 goals during the season! Joking apart, they create so many chances any striker worth his money would thrive on the service they provided.

We are back on the map now and, inevitably, people will be asking where we go from here. I think we will do all right. It'll be tough and I don't think we should get over-ambitious but we are more than capable of finishing in the top ten.

I think Wolves have exceeded what Fosun could realistically have expected by this stage of their ownership, and they'll need to understand that it takes time to adjust to the top level but, from what I hear around the club, they are in it for the long run and are not the type of people to accept second best.

The fans are excited and I share that enthusiasm. I love being part of Nuno's 'Pack'. We've waited a long time for this, so long may it continue.

Steve Bull MBE
Vice-President, Wolverhampton Wanderers FC

INTRODUCTION

Nuno Teve Um Sonho (Nuno Had a Dream)

Nuno had a dream,
To build a football team,
With Chinese owners and a wonder kid from Porto,
Five at the back and pace in attack,
We're Wolverhampton – we're on our way back.

Never in their wildest dreams would even the most ardent Wolves supporters envisage what was to unfold over the 2017-18 season. The club was hardly mentioned in the campaign preamble when promotion candidates were being discussed. On the contrary, the sceptics were out in force. What chance would Wolves have with a Portuguese coach with no experience of English football, let alone the fierce and relentless demands of the country's second tier?

Even more baffling was the fact the man charged with constructing a successful season by the club's owners, the Fosun International Group, was a former goalkeeper. Never mind that Nuno Espírito Santo had coached at the highest level of European football. He would, claimed the experts, be swallowed up and eaten alive by his battle-hardened competitors in the Championship.

The arrival of overseas recruits Rúben Neves, Diogo Jota, Léo Bonatini, Alfred N'Diaye and Willy Boly – to add to already recruited Ivan Cavaleiro, Romain Saïss and Hélder Costa –brought further scorn, poured with relish on Wolves' chances. All these overseas players wouldn't be able to cope with the unrelenting fixture schedule or the harsh and draining excesses of the British winter – or so the pundits and rival managers claimed, but Nuno's dream was not built on imported quicksand.

As well as the overseas players, there was a solid foundation of home-based signings, John Ruddy, Ryan Bennett and Barry Douglas added to the rejuvenated input of a newly adventurous Matt Doherty, and Conor Coady – now remodelled as a third centre back and on-field leader.

There was a new system too – 5-4-1 in its simplest terms – a flexible, fluid line-up with free-flowing, attractive football at its core, but it was not just about a formation. It was about a philosophy and

A triumphant Nuno emerges through the smoke as the fans jostle for a photo.

a trust in Nuno's ethics of hard work and a focus, not on long-term aims but a match-by-match obsession.

It all began rather tamely with 1-0 victory against newly-relegated Middlesbrough, but this was a mere taster of better things to come. There have been many false dawns at the club but not this time. Any nagging doubts were blown away like the smoke from the pre-match Molineux fireworks.

The pyrotechnics continued on the pitch in an explosion of expansive football, the likes of which Wolves fans of modern times had never witnessed. Once Wolves hit the top of the Championship at the end of October they stayed there until the end of the season when the title was lifted. The winter months came and went without interrupting the team's glorious journey to the Premier League, remaining undefeated in November and December. So much for faint-hearted foreigners.

There were blips along the way but one of the strengths of Nuno's team was the ability to bounce back from defeats with a renewed, steely endeavour without losing sight of the need to play football the right way.

The snipers were out in force when rival clubs launched a campaign to have Wolves investigated by the English Football League (EFL) over their alleged irregular involvement with the super-agent Jorge Mendes who, as well as being Nuno's agent, had brought some of the overseas players to Molineux. Fosun and Wolves provided all the relevant information, which had already been approved at the time of the original takeover by both the EFL and the Football Association (FA). After the formal inquiry Wolves were cleared of all the accusations and the season continued down its unstoppable route towards promotion.

There was drama, spilling over with emotion, notably with the late, late winner against Bristol City, with Nuno having been banished from the touchline to celebrate in the home directors' box. There was the nine-man victory at Middlesbrough and the slightly unreal double missed penalty finale at Cardiff City.

Then there was what has become known as THE goal, scored by the 'wonder kid from Porto', Rúben Neves – the screaming volley against Derby which remains embedded in everyone's minds.

I travelled to the Derby game on public transport and an hour after the final whistle, waiting at the bus stop, fans were still enthusing about it and replaying footage on their mobile phones. It was almost as if they could not quite believe what they had just witnessed. If the passion and celebrations on the touchline from Nuno and his staff were unrestrained then it was matched among the fans.

That was probably one of Nuno's greatest achievements. He created a unique, unflinching and unbreakable bond with Wolves supporters which has gone from strength to strength and remains impenetrable. The sell-out crowds warmed not just to his football but the joyous way he embraced and shared their love for their club. It was a two-way love affair.

Before the final home game of the season, when the trophy was lifted after the 0-0 draw against Sheffield Wednesday, the fans lined the streets around Molineux to welcome their heroes through the mists of orange smoke flares. Through it emerged Nuno and his players to acknowledge the rapturous and deserved acclaim.

The dream came true but you sensed it has not ended. The Premier League awaits and Nuno and his team face fresh and more daunting challenges. The Fosun owners have indicated they are not merely happy to consolidate and survive in the top flight. They mean business and have the investment ready to back up their ambitions.

Wolves have been here before, of course, having won promotion to the Premier League in 2003 and 2009 under the ownership of Sir Jack Hayward and Steve Morgan and the management of Dave Jones and Mick McCarthy.

This time, though, it feels different. There is an optimism, supported by an unflinching ambition of the owners and manager and reinforced by an acceptance that more and sizeable investment will be needed.

Who knows where it might end? It promises to be an exhilarating journey and Wolves fans are ready to hop on board.

1

The Dream Maker

"I hope I can build a new future here."
Nuno Espírito Santo

Who? That was the question most Wolves fans were asking when it was announced at the start of the season that Nuno Espírito Santo had been recruited by the club's owners. The Molineux faithful had been force-fed a diet of foreigners in the past who had not lived up to the high expectations their appointments had generated.

What's more, he was a former goalkeeper and one with a fairly undistinguished playing pedigree at club level, though he did feature for his country at the 1996 Olympic Games when Portugal finished fourth. However, a detailed study of his coaching career would reveal that here was a man of real substance and widespread experience, albeit with a few blemishes which had brought criticism and sackings along the way.

The arrival of Nuno, as he had become known, was hardly a surprise when it was revealed he was the first player recruited by the super-agent Jorge Mendes, whose Gestifute agency had been a crucial part of the Fosun takeover of Wolves. It has been widely reported that Nuno and Mendes first met in a Portuguese nightclub when the goalkeeper was just 22 years old. They have retained strong links ever since.

Nuno had enjoyed relative success at minnows Rio Ave when he moved into coaching, and guided them to two Portuguese cup finals, but was relatively unknown outside his homeland. A move into the big-time took him to Valencia in 2014, in an appointment that was shrouded in controversy with accusations that he was only taken on by them because of Mendes' links to club owner Peter Lim.

His stint at the Spanish club began in a blaze of glory and he eventually steered them to fourth place in his first season, the highlights of which included a 2–1 home win and a 2–2 away draw against Real Madrid, and he was named *La Liga* manager of the month three times.

Nuno with his staff and their families.

The high quickly turned to a low as, a few months into the following season after Valencia slumped to ninth place, the fans turned against him and he was sacked.

"I was Valencia coach for 500 days and took them into the Champions League," said Nuno at the time. "It was an important mark in my career. I was sad to leave, but at that level demands are high. I didn't feel hurt by the fans. We had a fantastic year beating great teams like Real Madrid, Atletico Madrid and Sevilla, but I was sad to leave.

"When I arrived at Valencia there was distrust. I and my staff had done good things at Rio Ave, but the impact of that in Spain was almost non-existent. The press questioned whether we were capable of taking on the project. They wanted the 'old school' with local people.

"I don't deny that what took me there was my friendship with Jorge Mendes. It's true that we're friends, but that doesn't overlook the professional side. If they didn't have confidence in my ability, they wouldn't have supported me. Those who weren't in the know saw it as using my connections. There were things that annoyed me, but some people admitted they'd been hasty."

A season at Porto followed but it was a brief and not always a pleasant stay, being relieved of his duties after less than a year in charge. Nuno faced more scorn from the fans of the Portuguese club and he was mocked when he

Nuno in typically animated mood on the touchline.

used a board to explain his tactics to the media after his team had lost a game against Benfica, and after a win against Arouca.

As he explained at the time: "It was a source of fun, criticism and analysis. It's a serious thing. I want to convey to fans the idea we have for the team and what we want to achieve."

Porto's loss was Wolves gain and his arrival at Molineux was marked by a clear, but what was to become a familiar, statement of intent. "I hope I can help build a new future here. I believe in the project. I believe in the ideas and I trust people." It was the beginning of Nuno's dream which ended in a runaway title win and the Championship Manager of the Season award, from the League Managers Association.

It was an exceptionally modest introduction in view of what he was to bring in due course but the fans immediately warmed to the way he embraced the club and the respect he had for Wolves and its history.

Nuno elaborated on the way he would approach English football during a lengthy interview with a website called *coachesvoice.com*. He explained why he would revolutionise football at the Molineux club and introduce a quality, the likes of which fans had not experienced in their lifetimes.

"When you think about Championship and you are offered a job in the Championship, the first step and the first thought that you must have is to say: Is my idea possible to work in the Championship?" he said.

"It's not about the Championship changing your idea. No. It's about your idea inside the Championship. So this is the first step that you make, and you say yes, we go. You understand?

"So I don't really believe that there is something different in the Championship because football is the game. It's the same thing. There are specific situations and characteristics of the Championship, but it's a competition. There are good teams, there are good players.

"So, you know, it's your idea. When we consider, we say okay, it's possible we go with our idea, with our philosophy."

That philosophy was soon to embed itself into the minds of the players, both those who were already at the club and those who were brought in, some at considerable expense, thanks to the involvement of agent Mendes. There was a style and a swagger about Wolves' performances but there was discipline too and a will-to-win even in the most difficult of circumstances.

It all stemmed from an indestructible desire by the manager to play the game a certain way. Not for him the up-and-at-'em style of direct football which was the traditionally accepted way of dealing with the physical demands of the Championship. There was also an acceptance from him of the need to be flexible enough to adopt his preferred style when opponents tried to combat the 'Nuno way'.

Nuno with his backroom team (left to right): Antonio Dias, fitness coach; Rui Pedro Silva, assistant head coach; and Rui Barbosa, goalkeeping coach.

"It's the way I see football," he said, in an end-of-season interview. "It's not that I invented something, a lot of teams play good football but it's the way I see football. If you have more of the ball than your opponent and you are organised and know when you are defending and when and where you will recover it, you are always in control of the game.

"Look at the goals we scored. There was a moment where we scored with fast attacks and the other opponents started to adapt. Then there was a moment we scored with set pieces and we won 1-0. There was a moment we scored with full-backs, two or three games in a row. It tells you we have solutions. It's not the style, it's the idea. It's the way we want to be.

"For me it [the direct approach] didn't make sense. If I have to adapt to the Championship and play like 70 per cent of the teams, I am not the right coach. The main thing is to have an identity. To have an idea. Go to the line and put it in the box? You come here and say 'no, we don't want that. We want the ball to come round again'."

The manager's attention to detail knows no limits, even down to the size and the shape of the tables at the training ground dining room. He had to handle a squad made up of players from 12 different countries who used five different native languages. To enable them to fully integrate, he regularly switched around the seating arrangements.

Fans with their Nuno flag, illustrating the bond he made with supporters.

"They had small tables and we had groups of English, African and Portuguese players. They divided themselves [by nationality] because it's nature," he said. "How are you supposed to communicate on the pitch when you don't off it? So I said: 'No, then it was tables for five, which was not big enough for all the Portuguese speakers to sit together. It stopped them sitting in the same place all the time. It was interesting to see how it worked, but they got the message."

Nuno is an avowed student of the game. He has an analytical mind which, ironically, stemmed from his playing career when he had plenty of time to watch and learn from the substitutes' bench. As he explained to *coachesvoice.com*: "I am going to be honest with you. I was a goalkeeper, but through my career I spent almost as much time sitting on the bench as I did playing, but this gave me two views, two perspectives. This allows you to see the game, to see space, to see everything. It helped me in the way I understand football now.

"My idea to be a coach came late, though. When you realise that the ball is faster than you, you say to yourself: 'Okay, I love the game. I want to go on in this game, but not as a player.' That is when I started to really think about the game. To learn from it. I spent two or three years in that process, of really trying to get inside football and look at my future."

There was also the influence of coaches he played under and there was no bigger influence than José Mourinho. Nuno said of the current Manchester United boss: "At Porto, under José Mourinho, we won everything with a fantastic group of football players. Mourinho built that. He made us succeed, win everything. This has a big impact. Later on, back at Porto, you get a person like Jesualdo Ferreira. So many years in football, and a man who makes total sense in everything that he says.

"There are other things too. I played in Russia, in Spain, I was a part of the national team. You take everything you experience, and it is like you put it all in a box. Then, when you need anything from it, at any point, you go in and you grab it. It becomes an instinct.

"Ferreira gave me my first coaching experience, at Malaga and then Panathinaikos. He had a very good team of people working with him – one of them, Rui Pedro Silva, is now my assistant at Wolves – but this is when everything changes.

"You join a specific philosophy. A view of how football works, but you add to this view and give these people your own view of the game, the view of being inside the dressing room. It is important to connect this feeling to the way you perform on the pitch.

"It is about sharing. One of the big things a group dynamic demands is to be able to listen and really understand, to learn from listening to others. You must always have space to share opinion, but at the same time be ready to make decisions that fit the way you think is better.

"This is when you recognise that you are ready to be a leader, to be the main figure of something. This is the feeling I had when I became a head coach for the first time. You have to win every game, and you work 24 hours of your day towards that. Nothing else happens in your life. You cannot relax. You cannot. It is all about winning and that pushes you, and makes you stronger. Really stronger.

"That doesn't mean you react well to bad results. That is exactly the same feeling. It's awful, and you hate it. That night, you don't sleep. You just don't sleep, but you have to be ready to go again the next morning, to go from that one step to the next. It is hard, but you perform better when you get the tools to help you disconnect. I am in that process. I'm able to disconnect sometimes, and just think about life."

Wrapped up against the cold of the British winter.

Such a deep-thinking, intellectual mindset was the essence of the man but, in stark contrast, was the emotional, sometimes volatile, behaviour he showed on the touchline, provoked by the sense of injustice he felt had been dealt to his team and his desire to defend them. His frequent outbursts towards referees and fourth officials saw him banished from the touchline on a couple of occasions.

He remained unapologetic about his excesses, whether his exuberant celebrations or complaints to officials. "I'm pleased because my conscience is very calm," he told the club's official website. "This is me, if I celebrated goals like I did this season, I'm going to do it again because the happiest moments in football are when you score a goal. That goal reflects all the hard work of a week, it's seven days for 90 minutes, so when you achieve it how can you not be pleased?

"At the same time, how can you not be angry when something goes wrong? It's your work, this passion that keeps moving, and I'm not changing."

Another part of Nuno's world is his relationship with the media. He greeted journalists at his regular press conferences with warm handshakes all round, but often the assembled gathering would leave, complaining about the lack of copy as his offerings were invariably along the lines of, "the next game is the most important" or "this is not about me or individuals but the work ethic of the team," or "I never look at the league table – just at the next opponents."

Once the promotion mission had been accomplished, journalists saw a different side of the Wolves manager. He revealed the fun side of his personality and explained he had been having golf lessons. He then showed the assembled media a video recording on his mobile phone made by his players and showing how they tricked him into playing an exploding ball off the tee which covered him with flour.

Despite his sometimes strained relationship with the media, Wolves fans hung on his every word and he was able to reconnect the club with them on a level in which he displayed both humility and warmth.

Nuno is a man of the people in many respects and his character stems from his simple upbringing. He grew up on the former Portuguese colony of São Tomé and Príncipe, a set of islands on the west coast of Africa.

"It was a little paradise," he once recalled in an interview with the Portuguese media. "I remember the beach, walking bare-footed. I remember my grandmother and my aunties cooking on the beach and all eating together on the sand. We left São Tomé after a coup in 1980. I went to live with my grandparents in a district of Barreiro (near Setúbal, in Portugal). There was no longer that freedom, of being able to go out without danger. In São Tomé there weren't even any cars. When we left the house, we had our feet in the sand. When we moved to the mainland I found myself closed in a flat, and that shocked me a bit."

Nuno started to play football at the age of 11 at a club called Santo Antoniense but admitted: "I spent a lot more time playing in the street than at the club. I've always been tall, so they put me in goal. I was the only one who could touch the crossbar!"

He joined Vitória de Guimarães at the age of 17 and recalls: "It was difficult. I didn't go there to have fun but to become a footballer. When you're young you feel immortal and that you can do everything. I couldn't. I started training early with the senior players and had the rigour of timetables. I realised I had to deprive myself of many things."

Now, as the man who has steered Wolves back into the big time, Nuno commands an affection which transcends the boundaries of the football club. His name is sung at every opportunity. There are stories of babies in Wolverhampton being named after him, women (and some men) have confessed an undying love for him and his face has appeared in tattoo form on the arms and legs of his devoted following. Fans have also been able to toast his success with a pint of Numero Nuno, a specially brewed ale from the local Banks' Brewery.

With his assistant Rui Pedro Silva, his constant companion on the bench.

Effectively he has become one of them. He talks of 'the pack', of which he is only a part, as an unstoppable force. "We know that having a pack behind you makes you stronger," he said during the season. "This is the spirit that we know. We need them and they need us so it creates a bond that has to reflect enjoyment first and also achieving good and successful things together."

The dream will continue. For Nuno, the 'project' is not some obscure desire to satisfy his own ego or personal ambitions. It is a deeply held belief that Wolves are a club which deserves to be among football's elite and he intends to take them there.

"I think the repercussions of the fact Wolves are back in the Premier League are felt all over the world," he has said. "It's a very big club that I personally think belongs among the best teams in England. The impact is all over the world."

Inevitably, there was a sharp stab of reality from the man and a reminder to those who were already talking of the club taking the top flight by storm in their first season back. The promotion celebrations were still in full cry when Nuno delivered a typical down-to-earth message. "It's about building and being able to create an identity," he said. "It doesn't matter the competition we're in.

"We know it's going to be tough. It's a big, big challenge. Everyone knows, but we are ready, no doubts about that. We've already started working, things are moving, the club is growing, the support of the fans, believing. I will keep my feet on the ground. We have to improve and work hard but we cannot say we are going to fight for the top 10 or fight forever. That will be a big mistake.

"We go to August 9, that's step one, then the next game. You cannot say what's going to happen in December. I am very cautious of what's going on. The summer is important, to have decisions on the squad and then we will see. "I am not obsessed about making an impression on the Premier League. I want to build a team who can play home and away the same – never change. Let's try to do it."

In a rare insight into his personal life, at the end of the season Nuno spoke about living away from his family who have remained in Portugal. "Most of my time I spend at home or with my technical team," he explained. "We don't have our families here, it's not easy, it's tough, I won't lie to you. They have their own lives. It would be a big mistake for me to be so selfish to take them away from their friends.

"I have big children anyway. They are at university and have their own lives – but we still see each other, it is two hours away. I live by myself (in Wolverhampton) in a nice place and I spend most of my time there, 90 per cent of my time there.

"I cannot tell you about living in England. I arrive (at work) at 8.30 or 9 o'clock, we train, we stay here until three or four o'clock, we go home, have dinner together. We live to work, if it was for the pleasure of living, you would not be a manager for sure."

Nuno can rest assured that he has a new family in the city of Wolverhampton. It is an enlarged group containing the supporters of the football club and many others. They have adopted him as one of their own.

2

Wolves' Chinese Dynasty

"We believe the club and the fans belong at the top of English football and getting there is our first and top priority."
Jeff Shi – Chairman, Wolves FC

Wolverhampton Wanderers Football Club has changed ownership many times over the last three decades. It has been handed around like a pass-the-parcel game at a child's birthday party, with each pair of hands stripping it of some of its protective covering.

After two spells in receivership, Wolves eventually landed in safe keeping when the prize at the centre of the parcel eventually came under the control of Sir Jack Hayward in 1990. There it found someone who would nurture it with loving affection until he felt it was time to hand it over. Steve Morgan bought the club from Sir Jack for the princely sum of £10 in 2007 and, after enjoying mixed fortunes at the helm, he decided to sell it on in July 2016.

Then along came Fosun International, who paid a reported £45 million for the club. The Chinese company's arrival at Molineux was greeted with a mixture of intrigue, suspicion and anticipation. Wolves' only previous flirtation with overseas owners was the infamous Bhatti Brothers era when the club was virtually run into the ground and close to extinction.

The business media were immediately able to discover that Fosun and its owners were not only men of substance but of immeasurable wealth. It emerged they are one of the largest investment groups in China with a chairman, Guo Guangchang, who has an estimated personal fortune of $7.3 billion (US). That's a phenomenal amount for someone who was born in a small farming village in 1967. He came from a poor family and his mother grew sweet potatoes to feed the family.

Fosun also have stakes in various leisure, entertainment, healthcare, fashion, tourism and property projects around the world including Club

Guo Guangchang, chairman of Fosun International and owner of Wolves.

Med and *Cirque du Soleil*, and in several UK companies including Thomas Cook.

The company's early pronouncements were encouraging, with Jeff Shi – the man who had led the takeover negotiations – saying, "We are delighted to have completed the deal to become the new owners of such a famous and historic club as Wolves.

"Football is enjoying a huge growth in China and, of course, is England's national sport. As part of our strategy, it makes perfect sense to buy a great football club. Our goal is crystal clear: we will do our very best to help take Wolves back to the Premier League as soon as possible and to stay there. We believe the club and the fans belong at the top of English football and getting there is our first and top priority."

Encouraging words, but the immediate events were less so. New manager Walter Zenga, who had replaced the popular Kenny Jackett, lasted just 87 days as Wolves slid towards the relegation zone. Julen Lopetegui, who took charge of the Spain national team instead, was Fosun's first choice for the job but the job instead went to the former Italian goalkeeper.

Zenga achieved just four wins in 14 games. He left the club in 18th place in the Championship and it was the 10th job in which he had failed to survive a full year. All four of his previous appointments had ended within seven months.

The Italian was replaced by Paul Lambert, who was in charge for 33 matches – of which Wolves won 14, lost 14 and drew five – and managed to steer the club onto safe ground, but left at the end of the 2016-17 season, complaining he was not given control over transfer policy.

A run of five successive league defeats in February dragged Wolves into a Championship relegation struggle, although they pulled well clear of the bottom three with five consecutive wins in March and April. The highlights of Lambert's reign came in the FA Cup, in which Wolves won at Premier League opponents Stoke City and Liverpool before losing at home to double-chasing Chelsea in the fifth round.

As he departed through the revolving door to the manager's office, he had made it clear he wanted the final say on player recruitment, an option which would not be granted to him.

The summer of 2017 brought a major restructuring behind the scenes. It was the defining phase of Fosun's planning and the beginning of the dream. Jeff Shi relocated from his home in China to live in Wolverhampton and Laurie Dalrymple stepped down from the board but retained his influential position as managing director.

Shi said at the time: "Since Fosun became owners of the club, I have travelled over from China on several occasions, and it has always been a strong intention that I would relocate when the time was right.

"It feels like the natural thing to do now, to move over to Wolverhampton, and to be fully engaged with the club on a day-to-day basis. I think this will help us to work together even closer, and make our leadership team even stronger.

"It is obviously a proud moment for me to become the chairman of such a great club as Wolves. Despite the season having its highs and lows, I have

Jeff Shi at Molineux.

enjoyed every minute of the challenge so far, and I believe we are well placed to make sustained and consistent progress over the next 12 months."

The search for a replacement for Lambert immediately focused on Nuno Espírito Santo, recommended by his friend and agent Jorge Mendes – a key figure in Fosun's takeover of the club – and what an inspired appointment that proved to be.

The agent was instrumental in many of the key Molineux signings with the likes of Ivan Cavaleiro, Hélder Costa, Willy Boly, Diogo Jota, Roderick Miranda, Ruben Vinagre and, most significantly, Rúben Neves, who was brought to the club, courtesy of Mendes' influence.

As Wolves romped away to the Championship title, the tie-up between Fosun, Wolves and Mendes became the subject of a major debate when several clubs came out of the woodwork to register their concern, claiming that the agent had an irregular influence on the club's affairs, despite not having made similar complaints as Wolves struggled through the 2016-17 season.

It was a matter of public record that Mendes had sold a minority share of his agency, Gestifute, to a subsidiary of Fosun in 2015. Further media inquiries revealed that Shanghai Foyo, a company majority owned by Fosun's chairman, Guo Guangchang, bought a stake in Gestifute's holding company, Start.

There was a link, albeit a tenuous one, but that did not prevent other Championship clubs expressing their concern, complaining to the English Football League (EFL) and demanding that an inquiry be launched.

A letter drafted by Leeds United, supported by Aston Villa, was sent to the League. Its contents included the following assertion:

No club may enter into an agreement which enables any party, other than the club itself, to influence materially the club's policies or the performances of its teams or players in matches and/or competitions.
Given the broad interpretation of 'agreement' in the FA's regulations, which can be any agreement, arrangement, obligation, undertaking or understanding whether oral or written, formal or informal or otherwise, I would invite the FA and EFL to consider whether Mr Mendes does indeed materially influence Wolves' policies or the performance of its teams or players in matches and/or competitions.

That rather wordy missive was reinforced when officials at Leeds and Aston Villa took to Twitter to take a further dig at Wolves' transfer dealings, with the Yorkshire club's owner Andrea Radrizzani launching an astonishing attack on the Molineux club.

We have our own problems but we should play in a fair competition. Not legal and fair [to] let one team owned by a fund whom has shares in the biggest players agency with evident benefits (top European clubs giving players with options to buy ...why the other 23 teams can't have same treatment?). We should play all 24 with the same rules and opportunities (it's enough to Google it). Congratulations to the best team but hope the league can be fair and equal to all 24 teams.

Villa chief executive Keith Wyness' offering was subtle but no less conspiratorial. He shared a story on Twitter about Lambert's sacking which highlighted his concern about Mendes' involvement with transfers.

All the complainants received a sharp response from Jeff Shi who, in an exclusive interview with the *Express and Star* newspaper, stated: "I was very surprised to see the Twitter from the chairman of Leeds because I knew him, I also had several lunches with him, together with Jorge! So, it's very strange. In person I talk to him and he's nice, so I guess maybe he has the pressure and I understand that. I was also surprised to see the Twitter of Keith [Wyness, Villa chief executive]. On Saturday I met him and said, 'What happened?'

"I'm the chairman of a club so I can understand the pressure. We're the guys facing pressure from fans and the league and I can understand releasing pressure on Twitter. On the other hand I think, frankly, it's laughable, because they know nothing about us. I know everything about us and our club and what we're doing. I know everything about the rules of the league, and the FA and the EFL knows our dealings, every transfer document, agent fees, all information is recorded in their library. Our opponents don't know much about us and it's not a fair dispute. It's easy for us to answer all the questions."

The Wolves contingent fill the directors' box.

Nuno's reaction, when questioned subsequently about the Mendes link, was typically blunt but emphatically delivered: "Jorge doesn't have any job here. Any job at all. You see him here? Come on. He is a good agent, the best agent. I am a client of the best agent in the world. I do my job; he does his job. We get what we need from him. If he can provide good players for us? Fantastic. If another guy can give? Fantastic."

Eventually this 'storm in a tea cup' was poured down the drain as the League cleared Wolves of any alleged breach of their regulations. The League were unambiguous in their insistence that nothing irregular had taken place, stating:

> *Following the commitment made in March, as a result of some concerns raised by a number of Championship clubs, the EFL has met with Wolverhampton Wanderers to ensure compliance with the requirements of its regulations.*
> *At that meeting, a request for information was made by the EFL and following a comprehensive review of the detail subsequently provided by the club, it has been determined that Mr Mendes holds no role at the club and, as such should not be categorised as a 'Relevant Person' as defined by league regulations.*

Wolves issued their own statement which said:

> *After meeting with EFL representatives and providing further written detail, a comprehensive review has concluded with confirmation that the EFL is satisfied there has been no breach of its regulations.*
> *We have always maintained our clarity on both FA and EFL regulations, which have been complied with explicitly since the change of ownership at the club in July 2016. We believe the release of these findings will bring to a conclusion any speculation surrounding the club's operation and extinguish any concerns held by other clubs.*

There were further issues raised about the transfer of Rúben Neves, who joined the club from Porto on July 8 for a club record fee of £15.8 million. It was to prove the deal of all deals for the 20-year-old midfielder, who was to have the most stunning impact over the course of the season, but complaints were raised that Wolves had acquired the Portuguese international in unfair circumstances and were paying him an unrealistically low wage.

Those claims were shot down in flames in a fine piece of journalism by an investigative website called *Arab News*, who were able to uncover the precise details of the player's contract and destroy the accusations that Wolves had got him 'on the cheap' because of the Mendes connection.

Journalist Duncan Castles revealed that Neves was paid €12,500 a month, after tax, while at Porto and although there had been significant increase when he moved to Wolves, Neves was still on less that the club's top wage earner of £25,000 a week.

According to the website's report, the League asked Porto for details of his earnings and the Portuguese club were able to confirm his relatively modest income, the equivalent of around £2,500 a week, meaning his Wolves contract amounted to a 'three or four times increase.'

Castles also revealed that Neves had played a mere 626 minutes of league football in his final season at Porto and had been rejected by a number of Premier League and Championship clubs as a transfer option. *Arab News'* findings concluded: 'The approach (between Wolves and Mendes) is logical, intelligent and long-term. It has benefitted the clubs who sign Gestifute players and the players who ask Gestifute to represent them. At Wolves it has allowed the club to build a team capable of holding Manchester City to a goalless draw on the Premier League champions' own ground then reaching the top tier itself on a controlled budget.'

Jeff Shi offered his own direct response to the Neves claims, hinting that Wolves were being targeted by other clubs in an attempt to sabotage their success on and off the field. The Wolves chairman said: "Why are you pointing at some players saying why are they here, or on a low wage, how do they know that? Some teams are trying to do something to undermine us off the pitch. If they want to do that we can fight back but I won't do that because

Jeff Shi with rock legend and Wolves vice-president Robert Plant.

I don't think that's the right mindset for anyone in the football industry. Football should be focused on the pitch, that's my view. I understand why they're doing that, to try and destabilise us."

It was inevitable that Nuno would attract attention from elsewhere because of the success and style he brought to Molineux and, sure enough, there was a confirmed interest – mid-season – that Everton wanted him as their new manager.

The rebuff was swift. "When we joined Wolves in the summer we came with commitment of something important, a big challenge," the Wolves manager said. "Since the first day we have been working really hard on that. The same thing that I ask my players is that every day is a day of hard work and only one focus, which is the club, what we want to build, how we want to perform. If I ask my players that, that applies to me also. There is nothing else in my mind and nothing else in the mind of the players. I am here to take Wolves to the Premier League."

As dust began to settle on the controversies and the season unfolded, there were inevitable claims that Wolves had 'bought the title.' The facts proved otherwise. They were, in fact, fourth in the spending league table of Championship clubs, with a squad cost of £41.1 million, behind top placed Aston Villa with £67.8 million and Middlesbrough and Hull City both on £62.7 million.

Super agent Jorge Mendes (back row right).

Nuno with his support crew (left to right): director John Gough, sporting director Kevin Thelwell, Nuno, managing director Laurie Dalrymple and chairman Jeff Shi pose for a picture with the Championship trophy.

It is clear that Fosun will – with the substantial riches available to them – want to spend even more to consolidate Wolves' status as a Premier League club, both for new players and a long-term plan to increase Molineux to a 50,000 capacity.

Laurie Dalrymple summed up the season's achievement and offered a glimpse into the future at the club's end-of-season awards night.

"The football on offer this season was at times like something never seen before at Molineux," said the managing director. "Fans tell me this is the best football they've witnessed at this club for 50 years and for that an enormous amount of credit goes to you Nuno and the backroom team. On and off the pitch other clubs provided questions, but we emphatically supplied the answers. This team, this club, simply never knew when they were beaten. For us, the hard work truly begins now. The hours of hard work (this season) will be worth it. It's a brilliant feeling looking out for the Premier League fixture list on June 14, instead of June 21."

Predictions of Wolves taking the top flight by storm and ridiculous odds set by the bookies of actually winning the title came soon after promotion was achieved. Just as predictable was Nuno keeping the lid on expectations without dampening the enthusiasm of the supporters.

Jeff Shi mingles with the Molineux fans.

The Wolves manager said: "We are one year ahead of schedule. That will tell you that they, the owners and Jeff (Shi), know that the Premier League is different and a big challenge. It is not my job to restrain their expectations, but just be realistic. If we can achieve what we want sooner, we will go for it.

"You know you are in the most competitive league, money-wise," he said. "In the Premier League every club can buy whatever player they want. We are not different. We've realised what it's meant, for not just the club, but the city. It's the surroundings and the people, it's making our fans feel proud to wear the shirt.

"This is what me and the players work for, we support each other and are proud of being part of something which is on the move. It's moving, it's growing, it's building. Things are changing, we have a big, big challenge in front of us. We go there motivated and will do okay."

Then there was a familiar refrain from the Wolves boss – the next game is the most important.

"Our expectations are simple. We have to bounce back from the last game. We lost the last game of the competition [against Sunderland], let's bounce back in the first game of the next competition in the Premier League," he said.

So the dream is not over. It is intangible and indefinable but under the Fosun and Nuno leadership, it will go on – and on, and on.

3

Pack Profiles – The Case for the Defence

"What a day, what a season, what a bunch of lads."
Danny Batth

A Ruddy Marvel

John Ruddy arrived at Molineux in July, 2017 with Wolves still in a state of shock following the announcement of Carl Ikeme's illness.

The 30-year-old goalkeeper, signed on a free transfer from Norwich, bought with him vast experience and influence which stretched beyond his shot-stopping ability between the posts. Before he started his Molineux career, though, his first thoughts were for Ikeme, the man he was effectively replacing, though he was being pursued before Carl's diagnosis was known.

John Ruddy saves the late penalty against Cardiff City.

John Ruddy celebrates his last-minute penalty save against Cardiff City.

"This is a bittersweet feeling for me – it is good to be here but the circumstances could have been better," Ruddy told the club's website. "Having played against Carl over a number of years, I know what a good goalkeeper he is so it would have been fantastic for the club to have had us competing and bringing out the best in each other."

Ruddy's value was immediate. His command of his area and his goal-line ability were a fundamental part of the Wolves defence.

Statistics can be manipulated and misinterpreted but in the Wolves keeper's case they were very informative. He topped the Championship charts with 24 clean sheets from his 45 appearances, and while Wolves failed to top the 100 points mark, Ruddy reached a century milestone of his own. He made exactly 100 saves over the course of the campaign.

An obvious single highlight was his penalty save during the dying minutes of the game, away to promotion rivals Cardiff City. With Wolves 1-0 in front, the Welsh club were awarded two penalties in injury time. Diving to his left, and with a giant paw out-stretched, Ruddy saved the first of these two spot-kicks, taken by Gary Madine, while Junior Hoilett blasted the second against the bar.

Ruddy admitted later his save was based on pure instinct as he'd forgotten his pre-match homework. "I did the research [on Madine] and then I forgot it," he said. "So, I went off a gut feeling and luckily I did because all his other penalties have gone the other way."

As well as his goalkeeping heroics, Ruddy showed another essential part of his skill set – his distribution – and this came to the fore when he became goal creator with a remarkable assist in the 5-1 home win against Bolton.

It was a measured clearance which travelled three-quarters of the length of the pitch and left Diogo Jota with an opening to score with a predictable calm finish.

Young Wolves fans have a cheeky request for John Ruddy.

The Portuguese forward admitted later that it came as something of a surprise attacking option. "This was important because we tried the long ball a lot to counter attack," said Jota, "but it's not supposed to be for John to assist. That's football and these sort of things happen, so we were happy."

A free transfer signing, Ruddy stepped up to the plate in the most difficult of circumstances and his addition to the squad was a tribute to a recruitment department, under the jurisdiction of Kevin Thelwell, which didn't always have to rely on the Mendes factor.

Record breaker

It went under the radar but Will Norris created a little piece of history for himself as second choice goalkeeper behind John Ruddy. The keeper signed from Cambridge United proved himself a capable understudy when he stepped between the posts for the cup games.

Norris kept clean sheets in his first five appearances and that included 120 minutes of action against the eventual Premier League champions Manchester City in the Caraboa Cup. He was eventually beaten in the FA Cup replay, 2-1 defeat, against Swansea City.

Will Norris in League Cup action against Manchester City.

His first League appearance was less commendable and ended in a 3-0 defeat in the final game of the season at Sunderland but in his seven appearances he did enough to suggest he has a bright future.

Just what the Doc ordered

During the 2017-18 campaign Matt Doherty was Wolves' longest serving outfield player and it was totally different to his previous seven seasons at the club.

The statistics tell that he made 47 appearances, stayed on the pitch a phenomenal 4,166 minutes, scored four goals and claimed four assists. What the figures don't reveal is how many miles he clocked up on his travels up and down the right touchline. They would have proved immeasurable.

It became a vital feature of Nuno's system to have two attacking wingbacks to supplement his strike force and Doherty filled the role to perfection with his tireless energy, sublime touch, excellent vision and the occasional goal thrown in for good measure.

The Irishman thrived on the additional responsibility handed to him by the Wolves manager and he took on his attacking role without losing any of his defensive qualities.

If there was one move which summed up Doherty's season – and Wolves' passing game – it was his goal in the 2-0 away win at Reading. He began it with

Matt Doherty and his family.

a header down the line to Hélder Costa, whose trickery left several defenders in a spin before he decided he had run into a *cul-de-sac* of defenders and played the ball back. It was then taken for a ride on a carousel of passing until it reached Costa again, who found Doherty arriving late in the Reading penalty area.

There was still work to do but the wingback cut inside a defender and fired a shot with his left foot into the net. It was a build-up of majestic beauty followed by an executioner's precise finish.

Doherty went on to score two more against Reading in the 3-0 home win. It was his fourth goal in four games against the Royals and his regal displays earned him a new four-year contract with Wolves in September 2017.

His contributions did not go unnoticed outside the confines of Molineux, either. Martin O'Neill awarded him a long-overdue first cap for the Republic of Ireland against Turkey in March 2018. It should be the first of many.

Thank you Norwich City

Ryan Bennett signed for Wolves as another free transfer from Norwich and was further recognition that the club was not entirely reliant on Fosun's wealth and Jorge Mendes's contacts.

Ryan Bennett challenges Man City's Oleksandr Zinchenko at the Etihad.

Laughter came wafting over from Carrow Road when the Canaries' fans learned that the central defender had moved to Molineux. These were typical of the messages posted on social media from Norwich supporters:

"Imagine having Jorge Mendes controlling your transfers and then ending up with Ryan Bennett."

"And perhaps the most bonkers bit of news of all, there are clubs actually wanting to sign Ryan Bennett."

It is safe to assume that the Canaries were not at their chirpiest after seeing the type of performances Bennett turned in, week after week, in a Wolves shirt. Ironically, he did not hold down a regular place in the team until he was called in to face his former club but, after that, he never looked back and turned in displays of great consistency on the right side of the defensive trio.

He made a total of 33 appearances in all competitions and showed the kind of calm assurance and intelligent distribution which was fully in keeping with Nuno's demands of playing out from the back.

There are moments during the season which scream out their importance, and Ryan Bennett provided one of them. It was the away game at Bristol

Ryan Bennett (No 5 shirt) turns to celebrate after his dramatic late winner at Bristol City.

City when he didn't even make the starting line-up but came on to provide a breath-taking finale.

Danny Batth's dismissal in the 14th minute forced Nuno to shore up the defence by replacing Leo Bonatini with Bennett. Wolves would have been more than happy to settle for a 1-1 draw against a team who were, at the time, considered one of their promotion rivals.

Yet, accepting anything less than a win was not in Wolves' DNA. The match was deep into injury time when Barry Douglas whipped over a free kick and there was Bennett to head in the winner at the far post. Cue pandemonium amongst the travelling fans.

"When I came on we were just thinking about holding on," admitted the unassuming defender. "To score the winner and see the elation of the fans and players was a great feeling. Those circumstances don't happen very often and it was a collective feeling of elation from everyone."

There were also celebrations in the Bristol City directors' box after Bennett's goal, but more of that later.

A powerful feeling emerged after that 2-1 victory at Ashton Gate that anything was possible from this Wolves team, and it was. Could it be that those Canaries' fans were now feeling as sick as parrots?

Leaders-in-arms – Nuno with Conor Coady.

Commander Coady

Nuno can be credited for some outstanding decisions, tactical astuteness and creative influence but none of them can possibly match the effect he has had on the career of Conor Coady.

The former graduate of the Liverpool academy had enjoyed a chequered career at Molineux since signing for Wolves as a midfielder and occasional full back, but the Wolves manager saw something in him which few others could have detected by switching Coady into the centre of his defensive trio as well as effectively making him his on-field leader in the absence of club captain Danny Batth.

It was as though he had been born into that role. He was able to combine a strength in the tackle, an ability to spot danger even before it happened, the skill to step out and start attacks and hit raking long passes, either to the flanks or to the front men.

There was an authority also about his presence on the pitch and you could sense he was carrying out Nuno's strategy to the letter as soon as the first whistle blew. A relationship between player and manager developed match-by-match and there was a piece of video footage at the end of one Molineux game which showed the two men embracing each other, knowing each had done their job. It showed a mutual respect, an empathy and a shared belief that needed no words. It was an emotional connection which spoke volumes for the whole club and its unity of purpose.

Every player has his personal moment to treasure and it's a fair bet that Coady's came in the 4-0 away victory against Bolton when the title was sealed.

The Liverpudlian completed 48 appearances over the season and was on the pitch for a staggering 4,305 minutes. He scored one goal from the penalty spot and what a special moment it was. The decision for him to take it was spontaneous and a nod of approval from Nuno was all Coady needed to step forward and take it.

"It wasn't planned," he admitted. "I never really thought about it. I'm not the type of player who's that bothered if I score or not, as long as we win and,

Conor Coady converts his penalty against Bolton Wanderers.

when we got the penalty, Benik Afobe got brought down for it, I just thought he'd take it and the ball would fly in the back of the net and it's 4-0, but I looked over to the manager and he was pointing and the boys were egging me on to go and take it which was a nice feeling. It just goes to show the character in our team and the team spirit, so to get that chance to go and score a penalty in front of 5,000 Wolves fans, because they've been fantastic with me as well, it was a really special moment for me."

There were more spectacular goals during the season and more important ones too but none was more popular than Conor Coady's penalty.

He was rewarded for his season's efforts with a new contract in September 2017 and was even mentioned as a possible contender for Gareth Southgate's World Cup squad.

"All the signs for him this year have been really good," said the England manager. "His personality and character is outstanding. He is certainly someone that, mentality-wise, fits into the way we like to work."

Coady didn't make the squad for Russia in the end but a hint from Southgate suggested that a good season in the Premier League might herald his first call-up. The England cap will surely fit the likeable and level-headed Wolves man.

Conor Coady with his family and the Championship trophy.

Another brick in the wall

It was a prominent female politician who once said, while referring to her deputy William Whitelaw, that every Prime Minister "needed a Willy". By that token so does every football team.

Wolves have a big one in the shape of Willy Boly, the 6ft 5ins, 15 stone 4lbs defender who became known as 'The Wall'. He was so christened by the *Express and Star*'s Wolves correspondent Tim Spiers, who at one point in the season suggested Donald Trump might want to ship him out to Mexico to fulfil one of his election pledges.

So immense was his strong and resilient presence on the left side of the defence, it was difficult to believe that Porto let him leave and move to Molineux on loan. The Portuguese club's loss was Wolves' gain and it enabled the defender to reunite with Nuno.

A product of French football's famous Clairefontaine National Football Institute, which also nurtured the likes of Nicolas Anelka and Thierry Henry, Boly was always destined for stardom, although, apart from a prolonged spell with Auxerre, his club career had been patchy. He'd turned down a move to Wolves a year earlier before joining in the summer of 2017 on a season-long loan, and has proved an immovable presence with a total of 37 appearances and scoring three goals.

Boly is another player who can deliver Nuno's requirements to the letter. As well as his defensive might, he is very comfortable on the ball and frequently steps out to launch attacks. He can deliver passes, long or short with Neves-style accuracy, and once insisted: "I really like to play this way, when the central ones have to go out to play, and when the team likes to have the ball. For me, it is not more difficult to play this way. I like and want to have the ball."

If anything, Championship football was all a little bit too easy for Boly and his lapses in concentration sometimes led to awkward moments for him and his fellow defenders. The Premier League promises to be altogether different challenge for

Willy Boly – strength and composure.

Willy Boly celebrates after scoring against Leeds United.

him but one he is more than capable of meeting. As well as his solid and impenetrable wall-like qualities, the Frenchman has also been described as a Rolls-Royce defender, which is fitting because he took delivery of a stunning new model of the luxury car during the season.

There are hidden depths to Boly's array of talents. He holds a *Baccalauréat Scientifique*, roughly the equivalent of top grade A-levels, in maths and sciences, and is adept at mastering languages. In addition to his obvious academic ability, he is a quiet and private individual off the field and it is a measure of his football prowess that he was selected by his peers, alongside John Ruddy and Rúben Neves, in the Professional Footballers' Association Championship Team of the Season. There is no greater recognition of a player's qualities than that.

Oh, Danny Boy

It cannot have been easy for such a loyal and dedicated club servant as Danny Batth to witness quite a significant part of the success story from the sidelines. The club captain made 21 appearances – 15 of them in the Championship – but it would undervalue his contribution to describe him as a bit-part player, because the Brierley Hill-born defender was still a leader, a powerful figure in the dressing room and a forthright and articulate spokesman for his team.

Batth took his place in the starting line-up during the early months of

Nuno's admiration of Danny Baath is clear to see.

the season and, while he would admit it is not part of his natural game, he worked manfully to adapt to Nuno's passing game and became a better player for it.

He still produced the tackles, aerial challenges and body-on-the-line blocks, though, which have been trademark of his Wolves career and his vocal encouragement was forceful and demanding. Batth's critics argued over the course of the season that he did not fit the profile of the 'new' Wolves and point to some of the errors he committed at key moments. The one thing he can never be accused of, however, is hiding away or shirking his responsibilities and he was justified in standing alongside Conor Coady when the Championship trophy was lifted after the final Molineux game of the season.

"I wish I could sum up how this feels, but I really can't put it into words," Batth told the *Express and Star* newspaper. "What a day, what a season, what a bunch of lads. Everyone – the manager, the staff, the chairman and everyone else – it's all come together this season and the fans are rightly loving every moment."

There is another side to Danny Batth which deserves just as much recognition as his football talent – his humanity and compassion, which once saw him selling copies of the *Big Issue* on the streets of Wolverhampton in support of the homeless. He has also set up his own charity Foundation DB which supports causes such as the homeless charity YMCA Open Door, and Football for Peace, which uses the power of sport to educate young people from disadvantaged backgrounds.

Leaders of 'The Pack', Danny Batth and Conor Coady.

Foundation DB also supports Yuwa Academy, an organisation that aims to keep vulnerable girls out of forced child marriage and from being trafficked. With his partner Natalie Cutler, Danny made a documentary highlighting the plight of young females in India.

Wolves and Wolverhampton can feel very proud of Danny Batth, the footballer and charity worker. He is truly one of our own.

Re-united with Nuno

Roderick Miranda joined Wolves for £2.5 million in the summer of 2017, which saw him revive his working relationship with Nuno, having previously played for the Molineux boss at Rio Ave.

He started the season as a permanent fixture and showed the stylish qualities which Nuno demanded from his defenders, but there was a downside to his game which the physical demands of the Championship were to expose. These were never more evident than during the defeats against Cardiff City and Queen's Park Rangers, where Miranda was given a torrid time by the more muscular threats posed by Junior Hoilett and Matt Smith respectively.

The defender also found himself in the eye of a storm during the season when unproven allegations surfaced that he was part of an illegal betting scandal while at Rio Ave.

Roderick Miranda with the Championship trophy.

Speculation that he would return to his native Portugal were regularly aired during the season but he stayed to share the title celebrations. He made 19 appearances, 15 of which came before the end of October.

In from the cold

A former refrigeration engineer who started out playing as an amateur with Scottish club Queen's Park before signing professional forms for Dundee United, Barry Douglas went through some strange career twists and turns before he came out of cold storage and arrived at Molineux.

After leaving Scotland he won the Polish League title with Lech Posna before joining the Turkish Super League club Konyaspor, where he helped the

Barry Douglas – on target against Bolton Wanderers.

club win the national cup. Wolves then plucked Douglas from this relative obscurity, paying a reported £1 million for him.

It was another transfer which belied the myth that Wolves had paid fortunes to assemble a promotion winning squad. The move produced such premature excitement within the club they inadvertently posted an interview with the Scotsman before the deal had been concluded.

There was also much relief in the Douglas household when it was completed. He and his wife Debbie had enjoyed their overseas lifestyles up to a point, but he admitted they often missed more familiar surroundings.

"People don't see all the sacrifices that me and my missus made by going abroad," Douglas told the Scottish media. "We missed out on a lot of personal stuff, like family birthdays, Christmas celebrations and times like that. So to achieve something like promotion to the Premier League is special. It's a lot

Barry Douglas celebrates with the backroom staff.

easier now for my family to get down and see us or get to a game. They've been a lucky charm for me so far at Wolves. Every time one comes to watch, I seem to score."

There has been one special visitor to Molineux – his granddad, Jimmy, affectionately known as 'Pops'. "My mum put him on the train at Glasgow and I picked him up at Wolverhampton," said Douglas, "but he's 83 years young and so dedicated. He got to see me score from a free-kick – those are the special moments. I dreamed of being a footballer as a kid when I was growing up with my Pops – to then do it on that stage with him in the stand was brilliant."

The one question which hangs over Douglas, who was awarded his first Scotland cap during the season, is why did it take so long for a major club to snap him up? His displays for Wolves as an attacking wingback are tailor-made for the system. His left foot is a wand as well as a hammer. He can drill home powerful free kicks or deliver inviting crosses for team-mates to score.

In 42 appearances he scored five times and created 14 goals for others which put him joint top of the Championship assists league with Aston Villa's Scotland international Robert Snodgrass.

It's taken him a while but the man who once fixed fridges for a living has now definitely come in from the cold.

Barry Douglas celebrates after scoring against Brentford.

Ruben Vinagre celebrates after scoring against Burton.

Waiting in the wings

Rúben Gonçalo da Silva Nascimento Vinagre, to give him his full name, was signed on loan from Monaco and made a quick impression as an attacking wingback with a turn of speed and an educated left foot.

He made 13 appearances, highlighted by his first senior goal in the 4-0 win at Burton Albion with the downside being his red card in the 0-0 FA Cup draw against Swansea City.

There were doubts about Vinagre's defensive qualities but his potential is unquestioned and, at 19, there is ample time for him to develop and fulfil the promise he showed as a junior in his native Portugal.

4

Pack Profiles – The Creative Department

"I love playing at Wolverhampton."
Rúben Neves

The wonder kid from Porto

Let's get the negative out of the way first. Well, by his own admission, his first touch was not great. As the ball was cleared to him, he flicked it up and it landed slightly behind him. The rest has become a part of history. Rúben Neves twisted, turned and with a wonderful mixture of athleticism, creativity, technique and ambition, he volleyed the ball into the top corner of the Derby County net.

Rúben Neves celebrates THE goal against Derby with Conor Coady in hot pursuit.

There was a moment as the Molineux crowd, stunned into silence, wondered if what they'd seen had actually happened. Then it was absolute pandemonium as THE goal was celebrated. It was still being talked about months later and will be replayed endlessly by those who saw it, either live on television or on the multiple times it was shown on social media and video footage. Anyone who thought it was a one-off fluke should be reminded that he recreated the goal to perfection with Jimmy Bullard on *Soccer AM*.

"My first touch, the ball went a bit behind me," Neves said after the Derby game. "So I had to adjust my body a little bit to get the touch, but I don't have too much to say because it was an incredible goal and I'm just happy to help the team. When you play, you have your characteristics, and one of mine is shooting from outside of the box. I have to improve, I have to take risks and I look forward to scoring more goals like this."

While on the subject of negatives, it cannot be overlooked that Neves had the worst disciplinary record of any Wolves player over the season. He served two suspensions, after collecting 11 yellow cards and one red. That is not the record of a dirty player but one who can be reckless at times and one that dives into tackles with an over-zealous desire to win the ball back for his team.

As far as the positives are concerned, where do we start? The £15.8 million club record signing from Porto has been described as the best player ever to wear the Wolves shirt, though supporters of an older vintage would suggest he does not come close yet to matching the '50s and '60s star, Peter Broadbent.

Neves was the focal point of Nuno's team, a midfielder who could start and finish moves, spray the ball with laser-like accuracy over long and short distances with the vision and imagination which are beyond the scope of most players. His six goals were all scored from outside the penalty area. He caressed them, curled them, powered them and, especially in the case of THE goal against Derby, volleyed one with astonishing precision and accuracy.

If further statistics are required, he made 2,677 passes and of those 2,273 reached their intended destination successfully.

Neves was linked with Chelsea and Liverpool before joining Wolves as a 20-year-old and it was inevitable that he would be linked with the major clubs again after his season at Molineux, but the midfielder, when pressed about his future, insisted he was not moving. More emphatically, once the campaign was over, he told the Portuguese media: "Right now it's not good for me to risk a way out. I feel very good at Wolverhampton, I have no reason to leave because I'm going to play in the best league in the world,

"The fans already know me, the club too, and everyone knows what I can do

Rúben Neves with his daughter, Margarida.

Rúben Neves monopolises the end-of-season awards.

for the club. I spent a great year there and I love playing at Wolverhampton. Therefore, I have no interest in going out, because it's the best for me and for my future. I came to evolve as a player and now that I'm maybe in the best phase of my career it would be a very big risk changing club. This is the right path."

Weighed down by an armful of individual awards, including goal of the season, Neves was also rewarded by a call-up into the Portuguese national team. He made it into their preliminary World Cup squad, though he didn't make it into the final 23 for the finals in Russia. For Wolves fans that was a relief. They were glad their midfield diamond would be fit, fresh and free from injury in readiness for the new challenge of the Premier League in August.

As if life could not get better, Neves proposed to his partner Debora. Needless to say she accepted, and as one Wolves fan suggested on Twitter: 'He probably slotted the engagement ring on her finger from 30 yards'.

Moroccan gold

If there was one game which summed up the contribution of Romain Saïss, it was the dramatic 2-1 Good Friday win at Middlesbrough, when Wolves were reduced to nine men after the dismissals of Rúben Neves and Matt Doherty. For the final half hour with the odds stacked against Wolves, the Moroccan midfielder literally ran himself to a standstill.

He had returned late from international duty in Africa but never shirked the task which became an uphill struggle for the last 30 minutes after Neves had been sent off. At the final whistle he lay prostrate on the pitch, completely exhausted.

Roman Saïss in an off-duty moment.

Romain Saïss collapses with exhaustion after the Middlesbrough game.

He admitted that it was sheer exhaustion, but was back in action on the following Tuesday, facing Hull City in a game which ended in a 2-2 draw. "We had a tough game on Friday and that may have played a part," he said after the Hull game. "To play nine against 11 (at Middlesbrough) was tough, and then to have another game today was hard again. However, we can't use this as an excuse. Every team is tired, because this is the Championship and it's the toughest league in the world."

Saïss had joined Wolves in the summer of 2016 but suffered a frustrating first season at Molineux, especially when Paul Lambert took charge. He lost his place after going to the Africa Cup of Nations with Morocco and had his own thoughts on his omission.

"I didn't want to create trouble so just carried on working, but at the end of the season it was important for me to ask the manager why he had left me out of the team for, strangely enough, basically the same amount of time that I had been away on international duty," said Saïss. "I knew the truth but wanted to hear it from him, but he couldn't tell me. He hid behind other excuses, which was a pity, but that's life and I just got on with it."

His career was rejuvenated after the arrival of Nuno and he found a role in the team which enabled him to complement the skills of his midfield partner Rúben Neves. He did a lot of the "dirty" work for Neves with blocks, headers, tackles and interceptions in front of the defence, but there is far more to his game than destruction. He scored four goals in his 44 appearances and was always willing to supplement the attack when the situation demanded it.

Saïss agreed that the new Wolves manager had provided him with the platform he needed to extend his career and enabled him to be called up by his country for World Cup duty.

"I realised straight away I was going to enjoy playing in his system and with his style," said Saïss. "I like running but not just for the sake of it. I like to have the ball and play. That's how it is now."

Alfred the Great

If there is one thing Alfred N'Diaye brought to Wolves during the season, it was a physical presence – and a big one. At 6ft 2ins, and a shade under 13 stone, it was impossible to ignore him.

The Senegal international was signed on loan from his parent club Villareal on August 31, 2017, and the close proximity to the transfer deadline made it seem like a last-minute decision to bring him into the squad. There seemed no rush to get him into the team, and his starting chances were limited at the start of the campaign. It was as a substitute in the Championship game against Barnsley in September that his first big impact was felt.

Alfred N'Diaye adds his strength to the midfield.

He came on as substitute for Romain Saïss in the 80th minute, with the scoreline still goalless, and he immediately set up the opening goal for Bright Enobakhare. It looked as if victory had slipped away when the Yorkshire side equalised in the 90th minute through Adam Jackson, but N'Diaye had the last word, sliding home a pass from Leo Bonatini with virtually the last kick of the match to secure the three points. It was the first of his three goals and the relatively unknown midfielder was the instant hero of the fans.

He was a massive hit in the dressing room too, hailed for his teamwork and his ability as a protector of the midfield and back line, often towards the end of matches when there was a need to close down the game.

Conor Coady summed up his contribution: "He's a fantastic lad, all throughout the season he has been there supporting the boys as much as he possibly can. Even when he was coming off the bench earlier in the season, he was still contributing with goals and changing games when he was coming on.

"I'll always remember the Barnsley game where he scored the winner at the end. I thought he was fantastic. It's things like that, that attitude you need, for the team to do well. Since he's come into the team he's been phenomenal. He's a real powerhouse. He runs through people and is someone who is massively important to the club."

You get the feeling he would run through a brick wall for his teammates and his quality earned him a place in Senegal's 2018 World Cup squad.

Alfred N'Diaye powers in a header against Norwich City.

World Cup winner

Morgan Gibbs-White has offered an exciting glimpse into Wolves' future. He has been carefully nurtured and man-managed by Nuno, who used him sparingly but enough to give him a brief and crucial taste of first team action.

In his appearances as substitute he has shown a skill level and maturity beyond his 18 years, and the Wolves academy graduate has grasped all his opportunities with energy and enthusiasm.

It is his presence in the white shirt of England which has grabbed most attention and he is already being tipped as a future senior international. He helped his country win the under-17 FIFA World Cup, netting in the quarter-final and final against United States and Spain respectively.

Morgan Gibbs-White receives his signed World Cup shirt from Steve Bull and academy manager Gareth Prosser.

Morgan Gibbs-White with his Young Player of the Season trophy.

Former Wolves midfielder Keith Downing, now coach to the England under-19 squad, believes there is no limit to what the Stafford-born midfielder can achieve. "We are excited as a nation to have these exciting players and obviously we are getting some recognition now by winning some trophies," said Downing. "I think he could make the World Cup in 2022. Morgan has huge potential and I'm sure Wolves understand that. Hopefully, like every youngster, he gets the opportunity to play at senior level."

Gibbs-White can be filed under the heading "One for the Future" – and what a future that promises to be.

5

Pack Profiles – The Goal Machines

"It was an amazing season, not just for me but for all the club. It was a season we'll always remember."
Diogo Jota

Costa bravo

Hélder Costa's season can be summed up as a campaign of two halves. Frustration was followed by an unforgettable reminder of his dazzling skills.

The club's Player of the Season in 2016-17 was hit by a serious ankle injury in the final weeks of that season and underwent surgery as the following approached. It left some observers wondering why the operation had not been performed earlier and, as he went under the knife, further questions were being asked as to how much he would be missed from the Wolves attack.

His return at the end of September was an anti-climax, with few signs of the nimble footwork and thrilling bursts of acceleration which had been a trademark of his introduction into English football. He is, though, an undoubted talent who had tempted Wolves to buy him from Benfica for £13 million – at the time a club record fee.

Nuno urged patience and caution during the season but was adamant the forward would rediscover his best form. "We all have to realise what Hélder has been through. That injury last season. Four months he

Hélder Costa celebrates after scoring against Burton Albion.

Hélder Costa in an uplifting mood.

was out," said the Wolves manager. "He didn't do pre-season with the team so he's doing his own individual development. Of course he's a player who has a lot of quality and we have to take advantage of him."

It was not until the second part of the campaign that the real Hélder Costa re-emerged. The fleet-footed, close control, dribbling and finishing were back. His contribution to Matt Doherty's goal at Reading and his two goals in successive home games against Sheffield United and Queen's Park Rangers in February provided the growing evidence of that.

Costa's only previous goal before those was a penalty against Leeds during his unfamiliar barren spell. In all he scored five times in 39 appearances but it is the foretaste of what more is to come from him which has so whetted the appetite of Wolves fans.

Hélder Costa and Diogo Jota share a goal scoring moment at Millwall.

The Bright one

Since he arrived at the Wolves academy as a 15-year-old from Nigeria, Bright Enobakhare has been touted as an outstanding prospect. There were ample reasons for that, mostly because of his natural ability, power and pace.

He has shown that ability all too inconsistently so far. His decision-making has often let him down in the final third of the pitch, but Wolves know he is a rough diamond who can only get better as he matures.

Goals in successive games in the League Cup against Bristol Rovers and the Championship game against Barnsley offered proof of his ability and were followed by some timely words of encouragement coupled with caution from the Wolves manager.

Bright Enobakhare – full of promise.

"It was his first goal for two years (against Rovers) and that is too long. It is too much time," said Nuno. "Hopefully scoring the winner will give him confidence and start playing catch-up. He was in the team to start the season but other players have now come into the team. The fact he showed the character after going out of the team to fight to get back in is good for us."

On the flip side of Enobakhare's season was his performance in the League Cup against Manchester City, when he missed two clear chances before Wolves went out in the penalty shoot-out after holding the Premier League champions-elect to a goalless draw.

Twice the young forward squandered opportunities to beat City goalkeeper Claudio Bravo and was honest enough to apologise afterwards. "I'm so sorry for the loss tonight," he said. "Only God knows what those chances I had means to me and I will not let you down next time."

There will be many more chances for him in a Wolves shirt – that's a certainty.

Ivan the Incredible

When he signed from Monaco, for £7 million, to become Wolves' record signing in August 2016, the initial reaction to Ivan Cavaleiro was not

Ivan Cavaleiro scores a vital second goal against Middlesbrough.

positive. There were encouraging signs about his skill levels but not about his consistency.

For most of that campaign the player, who had made 63 appearances for Portugal at junior levels, failed to live up to either his reputation or his fee and he finished the season with five goals from 31 appearances.

What a difference Nuno made. After the new manager arrived, the real Cavaleiro suddenly surfaced in an explosion of power and strong running mixed with subtlety and intricacy. His nine goals from 46 appearances (coupled with 13 assists which put him third behind Barry Douglas and Robert Snodgrass in the Championship table) came in various shapes and sizes – long range curlers, tap-ins and even a header in the 2-1 win at Middlesbrough.

A personal favourite was his goal in the 2-0 away win at Reading. He started the move with a pass to Diogo Jota and finished it by rolling his foot over the top of the ball to bamboozle goalkeeper Vito Mannone and stroke it into the net. It was a finish of pure impudence from a player on top of his game.

His mood was reflected in an interview he gave to Portuguese paper *Record*: "It's the result of the work I've been doing in recent months, but it's also thanks to my teammates. This motivates me even more to continue working and improving. I believe this is the best moment of my career since I arrived in England. I felt some difficulties of adaptation in the first season, in which I suffered several injuries. This year I have managed to make more games as a starter and play at a good level."

Cavaleiro also stressed the importance Nuno had made to his career: "He told me he wanted to help me grow as a player and make a better season than the last. He's been a very important person to me. He and his technical staff – they are all concerned with our physical and personal wellbeing. Fortunately, it has gone very well. We understand each other in attack, I hope it continues."

Wolves fans hope so too. He has convinced them after their first-season reservations.

Going up! – Ivan Cavaleiro and Hélder Costa.

Diogo not Diego

It is difficult to know where to start with Diogo Jota, such has been his profound impact. He was signed on loan from Atlético Madrid at the start of the season as another of Nuno's chosen ones, having worked with him at Porto and, after coming to terms with his first name spelling, Wolves fans did not have to wait too long before recognising what a talent he was. At the finish of the campaign he had netted 18 goals from 46 appearances and provided five assists.

Another revealing fact was that he was fouled no fewer than 95 times in Championship games. He was no shrinking violet, however, and he, in return, committed 71 fouls himself and was booked nine times.

The physical side of the League was a severe test for the slightly-built Jota, who,

Diogo Jota provides a composed finish against Bolton Wanderers.

like many of the other overseas players had never experienced a season of such demanding intensity. He was often singled out for early treatment by opposition players and that regularly turned Nuno into a raging wreck on the sidelines because he was so infuriated by what he argued was a lack of protection for his main forward.

The physical demands began to take their toll on Jota as the season progressed, especially when he suffered an ankle injury in the 3-0 home win against Reading in an incident that went unpunished by the referee. Jota made his personal feelings known when he posted a picture on Instagram of his swollen ankle with the caption 'no words and no card', but he was back on the goal trail to score four goals in a five-game sequence on his return, and his delight in reaching the Premier League was unrestrained.

"It's a dream come true, I always watched the Premier League as a kid and I'm really looking forward to it and I'll do my best," he said. "I said in my first interview I want to contribute with assists and goals, because that's what my position requires. I know I can have a chance from a few yards or long yards, I have to take advantage from every chance I get to score. Fortunately, I was

Diogo Jota with his top goals scorer award.

able to participate in a good amount of goals, but the most is important is we reached our goal of promotion. It was an amazing season, not just for me but for all the club. It was a season we'll always remember."

Wolves announced, in January 2018, that they would sign the 21-year-old on a permanent deal at the end of the season with chairman Jeff Shi telling the club's website: "As a management group, our aim is to provide the head coach with a playing squad that gives him the best possible chance to succeed and I believe Diogo is certainly a player that does that, and will continue to do that beyond this season."

A scout from a Premier League club was a regular visitor to Molineux with instructions to monitor Jota. I asked him if he was good enough to play at the top level and the reply was: "Yes, but I'm not sure where you would play him."

Wolves had the answer to that particular teaser. Jota could play anywhere it was possible for him to hurt opposing defences.

Brazilian blend

During the summer of 2017, from the obscurity of Al-Hilal FC in Saudi Arabia, came Léo Bonatini on a season-long loan and it ended Wolves' search for a striker. Initially it raised a few eyebrows of puzzlement, but that didn't last long.

The Brazilian hit the ground running, scoring on his debut in the opening game of the season against Middlesbrough. It was the only goal in a 1-0 victory and he went on to score 12 goals in his first 20 games. At one point he was the Championship's top marksman but following the feast came the famine and, after netting the only goal in a 1-0 win at Birmingham City in December, Bonatini failed to score again all season.

There was more to his game than goals and he was the perfect striker for the Nuno system, with his ability to receive the ball, shield it and bring others into play. Inevitably, though, as with most strikers, his lack of goals seemed to drain his confidence and he lost his regular place.

The adjustment the Brazilian faced after playing in Saudi Arabia was enormous but he relished the challenge. "Here, they kick more, they press more and they don't let us play," he told Sky Sports. "It is different. Not every contact is a foul. They let the game flow, which is nice, and it is as if the fans are playing with us. We feel it."

Wolves fans warmed to Bonatini and towards the end of the season they were willing him to score a goal. Though his goal drought continued, they have recognised the contribution he made.

Leo Bonatini (centre) in celebratory mood with Barry Douglas and Rúben Neves.

The loan ranger

He arrived back at Molineux in floods of tears – tears of joy. Benik Afobe was returning to Wolves on loan from Bournemouth, just before the January transfer window slammed shut and it turned him into a nervous wreck.

"It was on, then off, then on, then off, then on again with 20 minutes to go, so it was stressful," he told BBC West Midlands. "I've had two serious career-threatening injuries in football before, but that six hours was probably the most difficult of my life because that's how much I wanted to come back to Wolves.

"I think I've played one 90 minutes this season in the Premier League, so it's been tough for me mentally but I've got good people around me and for me to have come back here it meant a lot. I was in my car crying when they told me the deal was on with 20 minutes to go because I knew there was no going back now in the sense of them cancelling or the deal not being on again."

He was welcomed with open arms by Wolves fans and after a slow start he did what he was brought in to do – score goals – and six of them came in his 16 appearances.

Afobe had scored 23 goals in 48 games for Wolves in his first spell at Molineux – from January 2015 to January 2016 – before he moved to

Bournemouth in a £10 million deal. It was that scoring record which persuaded Wolves to take him back on loan after Leo Bonatini's goals dried up and Afobe repaid that faith handsomely with some match-winning displays.

There was a bizarre twist to the Afobe story when he signed a permanent contract at the end of the season, but was shipped out to Stoke City less than two weeks later in a loan move with the promise of a permanent deal in January 2019.

There were those who argued that he could not play the 'Nuno way' and was not able to participate ably enough in the build-ups. That part of his game certainly improved in his second spell at the club, but his true worth can be measured in those six goals which helped Wolves cross the line into the Premier League.

They also played their part

Dave Edwards made three appearances in all competitions, Nouho Dicko played seven times and scored twice, Rafa Mir made four appearances, Jordan Graham three, Ben Marshall nine, Michał Zyro two, Jack Price nine, Connor Ronan seven, Kortney Hause four, Sylvain Deslandes three and Donovan Wilson two. Goalkeeper Harry Burgoyne also made a 19-minute appearance as substitute in the final game of the season at Sunderland.

There was also a sensational debut for Oskar Buur Rasmussen who scored a late equaliser against Hull after coming on as sub, one of two appearances made by the young Dane.

All smiles from Benik Afobe.

Benike Afobe and Willy Boly on the city tour parade with Championship trophy.

6

The Game Changers

"I don't look at the league table. I look game by game."
Nuno Espírito Santo

There were many landmark incidents and matches over the 2017-18 season which pointed the way to the Championship title. Here we capture the highlights and decisive moments of a memorable campaign.

Saturday August 5, 2017 – Wolves 1 Middlesbrough 0

A near-capacity crowd of 29,692 came with eager anticipation to see the new-look Wolves and left with a taste – but only a brief one – of what was to come. A new coach with seven new signings in his first game started with a win and while it was not always a convincing one it was a more-than-satisfying appetiser.

Nuno gave debuts to newcomers John Ruddy, Roderick Miranda, Willy Boly, Rúben Neves, Barry Douglas, Diogo Jota and Léo Bonatini, so it was never going to be a fluent team display. Likewise, Boro boss Gary Monk also gave first starts to six players from his expensively assembled team, including £15 million striker Britt Assombalonga, and there was very much a 'first day of term' feel to the match.

It was Bonatini who announced himself to the Molineux fans with a debut goal as he latched onto a loose pass from Daniel Ayala before slotting his shot past Darren Randolph, while goalkeeper

Willy Boly shows his strength against Boro's Britt Assombalonga and Cyrus Christie.

Ruddy also made a good first impression with a fine late save from Assombalonga as Boro pressed for an equaliser.

More significantly, the home supporters got their first glimpse of the wonder kid from Porto. Neves had the crowd drooling over his range of passing and his team-mates too. His new teammates were also impressed, with Matt Doherty describing one particular pass like this: "He'd hit quite a few of those passes against Leicester in pre-season but the one against Middlesbrough didn't even get that far off the ground. It was like a bullet. I think that's when the fans realised he had a serious passing range. I was getting tagged in videos for quite a while after that."

The workmanlike team performance was greeted with what was to become a familiar response from the manager. It was good but he was already demanding more.

"It was a tough game and in the first half we played very well," said Nuno. "We controlled the game and this is the way we should work. I think that we deserved

Léo Bonatini celebrates his debut goal.

the three points and we are pleased with the boys. We are still not the final product and every game will be better. This is the line that we want from the boys, always progress, always get better.

"We knew that today was a special day for all of us. We want to thank the fans and build this engagement between the team and the fans because Molineux is going to be a very difficult place for opponents. The victory gives us the confidence to work but we have to work harder. There is no perfection in football. You have to improve every day. You can do anything you want but if you don't have the heart there is no point."

The heart and soul of the new Wolves was beginning to take shape.

August 12, 2017 – Derby County 0 Wolves 2

The Championship season was only a week old, yet the dream was already beginning to develop. There were 2,500 Wolves fans at Pride Park, soaking up the sunshine and the joy of their team's football.

Barry Douglas celebrates his first goal for Wolves.

Sandwiched between the Derby game and opening day win against Boro was a 1-0 League Cup win against Yeovil Town, meaning that Nuno became the first Wolves manager since Ronnie Allen in 1965 to win his first three games in charge. Forget the statistics, though, it was the quality of the football which was so enthralling. It was brimming with style but with a hard edge to it which ensured a third successive clean sheet.

The emerging wingback play of Matt Doherty and Barry Douglas began to sparkle and the Scotsman's deadly left foot brought him his first goal with a cross-shot which flew in off Derby defender Richard Keogh in the 32nd minute. Wolves' growing dominance in the second half should have brought them further goals but they had to settle for one more. It was delightfully constructed, with Bright Enobakhare finding Diogo Jota who provided Ivan Cavaleiro with a simple tap-in.

Inevitably Nuno was in an even more demanding frame of mind after the match and the third successive clean sheet pleased him as much as the third straight victory.

Diogo Jota crosses for Ivan Cavaleiro to score Wolves' second goal.

"From day one they knew what we wanted but the talent must be supported by a lot of discipline," he said. "The boys have this culture of working to get better each day. The spaces were in the Derby team. We should have taken advantage sooner. The chances were there and the goals will come, but defending well is important and clean sheets are a first step to winning. We always start from the back. It's important to build a team from there and be solid and balanced and the boys are getting the message."

The fans were getting the message too. Something was happening with Wolves and they were beginning to understand what it meant.

August 19, 2017 – Wolves 1 Cardiff City 2

It was the first true test of whether Wolves could handle the more physical side of the Championship and they were taught a lesson by Neil Warnock's team. The Bluebirds were also flying high and, like Nuno's team, had won their opening three games. It was a tight, tense and tough encounter and Wolves were always second best in the battles that mattered.

After a scoreless first half, Cardiff went ahead a minute after the break through Joe Rails and though Léo Bonatini levelled after a mistake by Neil

Wolves players complain to referee Scott Duncan as Romain Saïss receives treatment.

Neil Warnock intervenes as Saïss continues the complaints.

Etheridge, Nathaniel Mendez-Laing, a former Wolves academy player, drove home the winner with 13 minutes left.

It was just as tasty on the touchline with Nuno going head-to-head with Cardiff boss Neil Warnock in a preliminary bout to what was to be the main event between the two managers later in the season. Nuno was aggrieved, in particular, by one challenge on Romain Saïss who appeared to be elbowed in the throat by Loïc Damour.

The Wolves manager was not happy. "Cardiff's game plan was to be aggressive," he said. "We have to be mentally strong to deal with this kind of provocation. We made too many mistakes for a team that wants to be strong. What makes you strong is how you get up from the big punches that you get. We have to be physically strong."

Wolves did pick themselves up off the canvas and went unbeaten in their next seven games, in League and Cup, in a sequence which included a 2-0 League Cup away win against Premier League Southampton. The run ended with a 2-0 defeat at Sheffield United on September 27.

They were proving to be a team that not only learned their lessons well but had powers of recovery which were to prove invaluable as the season progressed.

Rúben Neves on the ball under the watchful eye of Nuno.

Diogo Jota takes on the Villa defence to score Wolves' opening goal.

October 14, 2017 – Wolves 2 Aston Villa 0

A win against local rivals is always one to be enjoyed, but this was one to savour even more because it took Wolves to the top of the Championship for the first time. The rivalry was revved up even more after the game when Villa manager Steve Bruce plucked and then swallowed some sour grapes after his team were soundly beaten.

Diogo Jota was in unstoppable form, yet Wolves had to wait until early in the second half before the Portuguese striker left a line of Villa defenders trailing behind him to score. Then Léo Bonatini added a second. It was not the margin of victory, however, but the quality of Wolves' performance which had even the hard taskmaster, Nuno, singing its praises.

"It was the kind of performance that puts you really close to achieving what you want," said the Wolves manager. "With no game of football are you ever comfortable as anything can happen, but we were in control of the game, threatening and creating chances. We were consistent in the way we kept the ball. It came for us in the second half as we did it so well in the first half."

Villa boss Bruce accepted that Wolves were the better team but added some sharp criticism both after the game and in the weeks that followed his team's defeat. For a start, he didn't like the way Wolves celebrated so jubilantly against his team who were meant to be one of their promotion rivals.

"All the phaff and all the rest of it, you would think they had won the Premier League after beating us," Bruce said. "We will remember that, while

Wolves' celebrations which upset the Villa contingent.

accepting on the day they were better. There is a long way to go yet. We're only a third of the way through the season. It's a long winter, and the crucial part is the winter. December is a big month and January is important, too. Wolves were better than us. They played very well on the night. The better team won, we have to be honest. Sometimes you have to hold your hands up and accept that."

Bruce, who was turned down for the Wolves job by the previous regime, will have needed no reminding of those remarks later in the season when Nuno's team went through the whole of November and December unbeaten. So much for these 'Johnny Foreigners' not being able to perform in the cold. Four wins and 13 goals scored during November gave them a firm grip on the leadership of the league.

Bruce then had another dig by claiming that Wolves relied too much on foreign imports and didn't give young home grown players a chance. The club's fans, however, were quick to point out that the Villa line-up was hardly made up of graduates from their youth development programme, while their reliance on more senior players was illustrated in statistics at the end of the season.

They revealed that the average age of the Wolves squad used over the campaign was 25.5 years which made them the fourth youngest. The Villa average was 28.7 which left them third from bottom of that age table.

More celebrations after Léo Bonatini scores Wolves' second.

December 30, 2017 – Bristol City 1 Wolves 2

A drama oozing with emotion, controversy and explosive incidents – this match had it all. Eventually it confirmed the belief that Wolves were becoming an unstoppable force at the top of the Championship.

It did not start too well, with the recalled Danny Batth sent off – in the 14th minute for a foul on Hörður Magnússon – by referee Peter Bankes who'd dismissed Conor Coady against Sheffield United earlier in the season. Ryan Bennett was sent on as a replacement for Léo Bonatini in order to shore up the defence after Batth's red car but more of him later.

Bobby Reid gave City the lead, but the sending-off of the home goalkeeper Frank Fielding for a foul on Matt Doherty led to Barry Douglas equalising from the resulting free kick.

Previously, Wolves would have been quite happy to settle for a point but Nuno's team do not settle for the obvious. Bennett rose at the far post to head in another Douglas delivery. Cue wild celebrations – especially in the Ashton Gate directors' box which was Nuno's vantage point.

He had been sent off for protesting too vociferously after Batth's red card and his fist-pumping delight did not go down too well with the assembled VIP guests. Nuno was in a feisty mood afterwards too. He had already been stirred

Danny Batth, sent off by referee Peter Bankes.

Barry Douglas and Matt Doherty celebrate the equaliser.

Nuno gets his marching orders after his touchline clash with Lee Johnson.

up by City manager Lee Johnson's comments that his side could do the rest of the Championship a favour by beating Wolves.

The Wolves manager said: "We don't fight against anybody, we are inside the competition, so this kind of message that Lee Johnson sends – 'let's beat Wolves to help the competition' – creates a tough atmosphere and that is absurd. People don't have to see us like we are something to beat. We're one team that wants to compete, game by game under the rules, for three points.

"So don't change the atmosphere. We're one more team – we're not the team to beat. I'm happy with the game, not all the circumstances of the game, people didn't do their jobs properly. Besides that we dug in well, the sending-off changes everything but we reacted really well in how we stayed organised in the game. What supports the talent is the strength and the power and the humility of the boys."

Nuno reserved another barbed comment for referee Bankes: "This referee, it's the second time he's had our game and the second sending-off. I think it's unfair. I'm fair. I'm sorry for my sending-off. I was sent off because he said 'you go inside of the pitch' – it's true I put one step, one foot inside the pitch and the rules said I should be sent off, but I was not rude. I didn't have abusive or bad words for the referee."

The victory stretched Wolves' lead at the top to 10 points. The bandwagon was well and truly rolling.

Wild celebrations after Ryan Bennett's late winner.

January 27, 2018 – Ipswich Town 0 Wolves 1

This victory at Portman Road was fuelled by vitamin D. The squad had spent the build-up to the game at a training camp in Marbella and the Spanish sunshine worked wonders for them. The trip had been pre-planned and was perfectly timed, as the previous game had been a tired and lacklustre 2-0 home defeat by Nottingham Forest. That meant Wolves had gone four games without a win.

A rare headed goal from Matt Doherty secured the points in a game which saw the team rediscover their attacking verve and defensive discipline. Many chances were created and the finishing touches were not always applied but they found Town keeper Bartosz Białkowski in good form.

Nuno stressed the importance of the Spanish trip – not just because of the weather but its added ingredient of creating an even stronger unity among the squad.

"They created bonds that are important," he said. "Besides the hard work they did there, the bonds and the time spent together away from the pitch, that creates a lot of things that are important in the competition. Sticking together, helping each other, that says a lot. They gain the credit that allowed ourselves to go and at the same time work and relax. Most importantly is the friendship they've built between them.

Matt Doherty scores with a rare header.

"It's a fantastic group in that respect. A lot of people say the players that came in would find it difficult to adapt and all these things but the players that were here before, this is the strong point of this, the way they received the new players and built this group of men that want to work and succeed together."

Would it be impertinent to point out here that another West Midlands club went on a mid-season trip to Spain with a rather different outcome? They went to the lively city of Barcelona, where some of their players faced allegations of stealing a taxi. They were relegated from the Premier League.

The win at Ipswich took Wolves' lead at the top back to 12 points, but Nuno would not be drawn on promotion prospects. His comments came straight out of his textbook response to such questions.

"I don't look at the League table," he said. "I look game by game. It was important for us but the next game is in our minds now. We have to realise where we are and be happy about that but at the same time have this sense that we still have a long way to go."

March 10, 2018 – Aston Villa 4 Wolves 1

The football world concluded that this was where the wheels had fallen off Wolves' promotion bandwagon. The biggest defeat of the season meant

Nuno and his players acknowledge the applause from visiting Wolves fans.

their advantage over Cardiff City was cut to three points, while Villa moved menacingly to within seven points of the League leaders.

There was no initial sign, during the first half, of the collapse which was to follow. Arguably Wolves edged it before the interval and went in level after Diogo Jota had equalised Albert Adomah's early close-range strike for Villa, but it was a different story on the resumption when two goals in five second-half minutes from James Chester and Lewis Grabban were added to by Birkir Bjarnason's late fourth.

Villa manager Steve Bruce was understandably upbeat after the game. "We played very well and we needed to against a decent team," he said. "It was a great advert for the Championship. There's 10 games to go and we've given ourselves a chance.

"Wolves have got some very good players. How they got here, that's another question that I don't want to get involved with, but we've got some good players too. We're a threat going forward and they all put a shift in defensively too."

On the other hand, Nuno was understandably downbeat. "We made mistakes we should not do and they changed the game. I organise my thoughts and I try to analyse. We try to see what went wrong and get it right for the next game."

There was an intriguing subplot to the Villa game. Three days previously Wolves had beaten Leeds United 3-0, which prompted a social media outburst

Willy Boly stands dejected as Villa celebrate.

Diogo Jota equalises.

from the Yorkshire club's owner Andrea Radrizzani about Jorge Mendes' involvement at Molineux.

Aston Villa chief executive Keith Wyness also chipped in with his own thoughts on the sacking of previous manager Paul Lambert but, as we have learned, all complaints were dismissed by the League and it was business as usual in the Molineux boardroom.

It was business as usual on the pitch too. The strength of any team is how it recovers from setbacks and after the Villa defeat, Wolves picked up 22 points from their remaining 10 games with their only loss being the 3-0 defeat in the final game at Sunderland.

As for Villa, after beating Wolves, they lost two and drew one of the next three games and that severely dented their automatic promotion hopes. They also lost in the play-off finals to Fulham and even worse was to follow for Villa when they faced a summer of financial uncertainty with the threat of a winding up order for an unpaid HMRC bill.

March 30, 2018 – Middlesbrough 1 Wolves 2

This match should have come with a health warning: 'Beware! Stuart Attwell is the referee.' The Nuneaton official was not top of the Wolves Christmas card list after his trigger-happy, previous performances in games involving the club, and those Molineux fears were well-founded with Wolves reduced to nine men in the second half after red cards were shown to Rúben Neves and Matt Doherty.

Nuno's team were well in control after Hélder Costa and Ivan Cavaleiro gave them a half-time lead, but what was to follow could not have been scripted. It was obvious that Wolves lost their heads but not the game.

The lead at the top had been cut to three points by Cardiff's win against Burton earlier in the day, and the Welsh club had a game in hand. Defeat against Tony Pulis' side could have had catastrophic consequences.

It was all going smoothly until Hélder Costa was through on goal and was brought down by George Friend. No foul was given and retribution was sought.

Three minutes later, Neves was shown his second yellow card for a reckless lunge on Friend and then Doherty was shown a straight red after clattering into the same Boro player's head with a raised arm.

It left Wolves facing the final 20 minutes with a two-man disadvantage and it drained them to the limit. Patrick Bamford pulled back an injury time goal and Stewart Downing shot agonisingly wide. The final whistle brought exhausted relief and Nuno managed to upset Pulis by forgetting to shake the Boro manager's hand as he joined his shattered players on the pitch.

Rúben Neves gets his marching orders.

Hélder Costa is brought down by George Friend to trigger retaliation by Wolves players.

Nuno celebrates, and upsets Tony Pulis.

The Wolves manager was quick to defend his team: "The players lost control of their emotions and I think it is the job of the referee to speak to them and calm them. My players are used to dialogue. The referee was not a dialogue person today. We are not an aggressive team that gets a lot of cards. What happened today requires a lot of analysis from us. When we had the same number of players on the pitch as Middlesbrough we showed we are a better team and they are a good side."

Pulis was not impressed by his opposing manager's behaviour. "I'd have jumped up in the air but I wouldn't have done it in front of the other manager, but that's up to him. If he wants to do that, that's fine, it's not a problem with me. He's not my mate, so it's not as though I've lost a friend."

When it came to upsetting rival manager, however, there was more to follow. Bring on Cardiff City and Neil Warnock.

April 6, 2018 – Cardiff City 0 Wolves 1

If the win at Middlesbrough was drenched in drama, then this was a piece of pure fiction, bordering on the supernatural. Stephen King would have struggled to make this one up.

Rúben Neves celebrates after giving Wolves the lead.

It was meant to be a classic encounter between the top two teams in the Championship – a clash of styles between Cardiff City's work rate and high energy, and Wolves' more stylish approach.

To be honest, it was a bit of a damp squib for much of the game. Wolves seemed better equipped to combat their opponent's muscular methods than they had at Molineux earlier in the season, and it was a stalemate for long periods.

The visitors looked in control after Rúben Neves delivered another free-kick classic, bent into the net from 25 yards for his fifth long range goal of the season, but the nail-biting drama was reserved for the final few minutes of injury time. Cardiff were given the chance to equalise when they were awarded a penalty for a foul by Conor Coady on Gary Madine.

Not for the first time that season, John Ruddy was Wolves' saviour. With a full-stretch dive to his left he kept out Madine's penalty which was destined for the bottom corner of the net. The relief was audible – but wait. Moments later, referee Mike Dean awarded a second penalty, for a foul on Aron Gunnarsson by Ivan Cavaleiro. Surely Wolves could not survive again, but they did.

Junior Hoilett slammed his penalty against the bar and the final whistle, which followed seconds later, brought celebrations on the pitch at the realisation that this was almost certain to bring promotion to the Premier

John Ruddy after his penalty save.

Junior Hoilett fires his penalty against the bar.

League. Just five points would now be needed from the last five games to make it certain.

What then followed totally trumped the atmosphere of confrontation generated during the fairly feisty game. Just as he had done with Tony Pulis, Nuno avoided the after-match courtesy of a handshake and ran onto the pitch to celebrate with his players. Neil Warnock was incandescent with rage and he marched along the touchline, effing and blinding in full view of the TV cameras.

The Cardiff manager pulled no punches in his interview afterwards. "I don't accept it at all and I think it's totally out of order," he said. "I think he (Nuno) was a total disgrace. I used strong words and I meant every one of them. He's got to learn that in British football you have manners and a bit of class when you've won a game. You've got to learn that, I'm afraid. I don't think I'll go into my office until after he's gone. I don't want to see him tonight if I'm honest. I thought it was a great game and it didn't need to end like that."

Warnock was more forgiving a day later in an interview with talkSPORT radio: "It's water off a duck's back now," he said, admitting the argument had exploded in the heat of the moment and that the two men had not fallen out permanently. "It's just one of those things with managers. You move on. I'm sure he will have learnt from it too. Life's too short, isn't it?"

Nuno and Neil Warnock before the fireworks begin.

The Wolves 'Pack' in full cry at Cardiff.

Nuno was full of apologies and accepted he needed to control his after-match behaviour. "I have to say I'm sorry," he said. "I was talking to an assistant and he told me in Britain we don't do that, but I've arrived here and I love this country and I love the football.

"Last year I was coaching in the Champions League and now I'm in the Championship and I'm very proud of what I'm doing. I want to be a gentleman to all the managers, I'm sorry to [Middlesbrough boss] Tony Pulis and I'm very sorry to Neil Warnock. It was not my intention to be disrespectful, but it's very difficult in the last minute when there is a penalty and your goalkeeper [saves it], you have to celebrate. I'm being honest. Once again I'm sorry and I'll try to avoid it."

In his assessment of the game, the Wolves manager added: "Football is always innovating and it's a fantastic game. That's why we love it so much. It can give and take. We deserve it. If you look at the game, we had chances not to suffer in the end but that's why people voted for John Ruddy in the Championship team of the season and he gave us victory. I was not even thinking about the first penalty (when the second was awarded) but we should control the emotions better, which is my job."

After the Nuno-Warnock sideshow had subsided, there were more important matters to be handled. Wolves were to win their next four games. Soon it was celebration time.

7

Celebration Day

"This is paradise."
Robert Plant

The celebrations began on a Saturday night in a quiet corner of a Wolverhampton hotel where the players were gathered before the following day's match against Birmingham City.

Nuno's team were watching the game between Fulham and Brentford at Craven Cottage when an added time goal from substitute Neal Maupay earned the visitors a point and mathematically secured promotion for Wolves. The nervous silence of the evening was soon broken with smiles, handshakes and relief that they'd finally reached the Premier League.

After the excitement had died down, it was back to business. There was a game against Birmingham to attend to and, with typical professionalism, they accounted for their local rivals with a 2-0 win.

Molineux was rocking that day – before, during and after the game – as it was for the next home game against Sheffield Wednesday. The title had already been secured with the 4-0 away win at Bolton, and though the match against Wednesday was a tame scoreless draw, the events before and afterwards were anything but tame as fans lined the streets leading to Molineux when the team bus arrived through the mists of smoke bombs to a rapturous welcome.

After the match, the trophy was lifted and paraded and Wolves' songs of praise were aired long and loud. The players' families joined them on the pitch for the fun and photographs. The fans were very much part of that atmosphere because that was how Wolverhampton Wanderers Football Club had evolved.

The dream was alive and so was the City of Wolverhampton on Monday, May 7, when Nuno, his players and backroom staff took part in a civic reception before parading through the streets on open-top buses. The sun had

Wolves players receive the Championship trophy.

Nuno raised aloft by his players

Players with the Champions banner.

Conor Coady and Danny Batth on the bus tour.

Rúben Neves receives the fans' acclaim.

Players on top of the world.

Fans line the streets of Wolverhmpton.

Tito Jackson with Danny Batth and Conor Coady.

come out and so did an estimated 80,000 people who gathered along the procession route. A further 30,000 were waiting at West Park.

The warm-up act for the 'Party in the Park' were former players Steve Bull and Matt Murray. Motown star Tito Jackson, of Jackson Five fame, was also there to join in. He had adopted Wolves as his team and they had adopted him as their latest celebrity fan. He visits Wolverhampton every month and is planning to move to the city.

It turned into a mini-festival as Wolves fan and soul singer Beverley Knight also entertained the crowd, and the local girl summed it up when she said: "It's been possibly one the greatest days I have ever spent in my hometown."

As far as the fans were concerned, however, the real stars were the players and manager, who also burst into song by leading their delirious supporters in a rendition of *Nuno Had A Dream*, and the huge crowds lapped it up like a congregation at a spiritual convention.

There was also a big turnout at Wolves' end-of-season awards dinner at the Telford International Centre, where fans and players were rewarded for their contribution to the hard miles they had travelled during the season.

A standing ovation was reserved for the inspirational Rúben Neves, who won both the Player of the Season and Players' Player of the Season awards, as well as collecting the goal of the season honour for his goal against Derby.

The top goal scorer award was claimed by Diogo Jota, who found the net 18 times,

Steve Plant receives his award from Steve Bull and Laurie Dalrymple.

making him the fifth highest in the Championship, while the Young Player of the Season award went to Morgan Gibbs-White for his World Cup exploits and role in the title-winning campaign.

The Academy Player of the Season award was won by Ryan Giles for his performances for the under-18s, and the Women's Player of the Season award was presented to Andrea Whetton for her performances and influence on the youngsters in the Wolves Women team.

Away from the football, the Rachael Heyhoe Flint award was presented to Steve Plant for raising funds and awareness for the Cure Leukaemia charity.

If it's rock stars you need they do not come much bigger than Led Zeppelin legend and Wolves vice-president Robert Plant, who performed his anthem *Whole Lotta Love*. The singer described his support for the club as "a murderous journey" but now he could confess: "This is paradise."

During the formal part of the evening, managing director Laurie Dalrymple brought some cheer when he announced the club were dropping their unpopular shirt deal with controversial high-interest loan company The Money Shop – they were subsequently replaced by global gambling company W88 – and he offered a glimpse into the future when he proclaimed: "We're confident that what we've seen so far is just the start of things to come as we strive for improvement. We are merely the custodians of this great club. I'm very keen to listen to fans, to hear what you think we're doing well and not so well – and where possible bring about improvements."

Robert Plant provides a Whole Lotta Love.

Sporting director Kevin Thelwell told the club's website that his work as the head of recruitment had already started as Wolves prepared for life in the Premier League.

"We need to make sure that we're capable of not only playing in the Premier League, but achieving something in the Premier League. That's the vision – to become a strong Premier League outfit," he said. "We want to be a strong Premier League contender which is actively playing in the top half of the league. The hard work has already started. It's going to be a long summer but one we're looking forward to.

"What we're gearing up for is to try and create a squad that matches the ambitions of our coaching team, players and Fosun. Their vision is to be a top Premier League team so we have to produce and we're relishing that challenge."

The final words of the 2017-18 season celebrations must end with Nuno, the man who had made the dream come true. In an emotional address, he was endless in his praise for everyone who had played their part, saying: "I will start with the ownership. I think we began something together and thank you for the support. The people that were here, Laurie (Dalrymple), Kevin (Thelwell), Matt (Wild, the club secretary) the staff at Molineux, everybody,

Nuno raises the trophy at the end-of-season awards.

every single person. The medical department, the kit men, and on and on, but special thanks to my team – we came from far away and we love it.

"Then the fans...they are everything for us, everything. This is why we are here. This is why we work. Honestly, from day one I felt something was going on in Austria (on the pre-season tour) when I had people coming to me. You cannot expect that, people coming from so far away to support you against a Polish team. I was surprised. From then until now it's been incredible. All the stadiums in the country, on Tuesday nights, cold, with the yellow ball. You were there and that means a lot, coming at the end of the game and celebrating with you.

"Finally I think it's the most important, this is the engine, this is what moves things – it's my players. I already miss you, but we begin June 27. You know what we have to do – and we will do it. Thank you – and now we have a dream."

8

The View From The Stands

"Nuno got the team playing a brand of football
I cannot recall seeing in 64 years of watching Wolves."
Steve Gordos

Wolves fans have shared that dream with Nuno and in the final chapter of this celebration of the season we have asked them to share their memories.

View from across the Pond

Andrew Wedge has lived every minute of the season and takes us on the emotional journey from his home in Oshawa, Ontario.

Andrew Wedge

As a Wolves fan of 50 years, I have experienced some amazing footballing moments. There have been plenty of tears also, none more than in 1976 when my dad packed up the family home in Wheaton Aston and moved us to Canada.

I had spent my Saturdays making the trek to Molineux with Dad to witness my idols like Kenny Hibbitt and John Richards when all of a sudden that green immaculate pitch, was swept from under me.

I have been in Canada for 42 years now and Dad and I have followed the Wolves with just as much passion and vigour as we did back home. Oh what memories! The 1980 League Cup final, Bully's goal against Scotland, the Sherpa Van victory, beating the big teams in the Premiership and how can I forget being in Cardiff for the play-off final.

I also have a laundry list of horrible Wolves moments, but I choose to leave them locked up in my therapist's office!

The 2017-18 season has been, by far, the most thrilling ride I have ever experienced as a Wolves die-hard. Besides stating the obvious about our abundance of new talent, two things have stood out for me.

Can anyone remember a season where our starting line-up remained injury free? I am sure every veteran Wolves supporter at some point expected some Paul Robinson clone to inflict a season-ending injury on the likes of Neves, Jota or Boly and, more importantly, we avoided those dreaded 'here we go again' Wolves moments that define every unsuccessful season.

In September, at home, a Barnsley equaliser one minute into injury time could have easily sent us into a spiral. Instead, N'Diaye pops up with the winner two minutes later, and how can you forget the Cardiff moment? Leaving the

Alfred N'Diaye after scoring v Barnsley.

John Wedge's funeral display.

Cardiff City Stadium with three points after conceding two late penalties in the biggest match of the season is not an ending Wolves fans have come to expect.

Our biggest opponent was our detractors, who only made us stronger. A certain Aston Villa manager said we wouldn't survive those Tuesday evening away matches in December. The man speaks with experience. Have you seen video footage of Steve Bruce playing midweek football for Birmingham during the 1997 season? It isn't pretty.

As excited as I am about promotion, this season was bittersweet. Seven matches in, Dad passed away suddenly. He was really excited about the start Wolves had made and he sensed times were about to change.

John Wedge gave me the biggest gift a father could give his son, supporting Wolverhampton Wanderers and, watching Wolves lift the trophy after the Sheffield Wednesday match, I pictured my dad celebrating along with us. I have no idea what heaven looks like, but on Saturday April 28th, it looked like the Bristol City directors' box. Dad was standing next to Nuno with a big smile on his face, pumping his fist in the air!

On the road with Wolves

Roger Vincent shares the thousands of miles he travelled with the Pack.

Never has the Wolverhampton motto 'Out of Darkness Cometh Light' been truer than in 2017-18. In the previous seasons we seemed to travel to away games not even in hope let alone expectation. It had begun to feel like we had no hope at all. Performances at home were so turgid that, at some games, we were the only two people in our row in the Steve Bull stand.

Then, out of nowhere, came Nuno Espírito Santo and yet another crop of new players. Having experienced the previous summer's false dawn of super-agent Jorge Mendes' influx of unknowns and the eccentric manager Walter Zenga, pessimism was still in the air, but an open training session was announced at Compton and on a scorching summer's day a few hundred faithful turned up to see if we had been mad to renew season tickets. As we tried to identify the newcomers, the sight of Player of the Season Hélder Costa training on his own did not bode well, without mentioning Carl Ikeme's unexplained absence.

Roger Vincent.

However, the team looked happy, the drills seemed fresh and the squad smiled for selfies with the fans and prepared to set off for warm-up games in Austria. Then, word began to filter out about the extent of Costa's injury and the terrible news about Ikeme's leukaemia diagnosis. We could sense more mid-table mediocrity on the horizon.

The realisation that something special was happening came at Hull. Rúben Neves thundered in his first 30-yarder and at half-time there was almost bewilderment among our travelling support, who all seemed to be muttering, "This aye the Wolves" – the style was just too good!

Despite our great displays, when March came around Cardiff, Fulham and Villa were still in with a chance, but then came the three most incredible games of the season. Down to nine men at Middlesbrough, we still beat the play-off hopefuls.

At Cardiff – Neves smacks in a dream free-kick, the Bluebirds miss two stoppage time penalties, Wolves fans collapsing through the tension and Nuno running wild across the pitch to Neil Warnock's disgust and our delight. Finally, promotion looked ours as Derby came to Molineux and that sublime moment as Neves conjured a ball from the sky and volleyed it into the net before an open-mouthed South Bank.

Rúben Neves celebrates with Digo Jota after scoring against Hull City.

The cake was iced with a 4-0 away win at Bolton – captain Coady stepping up to take the penalty that sealed the title, setting up Nuno's joyous sprint across Molineux with the Championship trophy the following week.

The Pack had done its job and for once the thousands of miles travelled by incredibly loyal fans were well worthwhile. This was the best I've seen since the 1950s and '60s.

When you are on the road with Wolves it is not always about the football. Millwall might be the most intimidating ground, but on Boxing Day we actually ate egg and chips in the cafe opposite the Den and felt welcome, despite wearing gold and black (it must have been the spirit of Christmas).

Finding the away pub packed at Middlesbrough, we ventured into the home hostelry, the Medicine Bar, and as the only Wolves supporters in sight were soon engaged in friendly chat.

A walk by the Thames cost us the chance of Jeff Shi and Laurie Dalrymple buying Jägerbombs in the pub at Brentford, but at least we benefitted from the club laying on much-appreciated free travel to a couple of games and subsidising the disgustingly over-priced Leeds tickets.

Fulham still have the best pies, but at the highest prices and, if you can't afford the admission fee, we found the amateur game on the park opposite Deepdale almost as enjoyable as the real match with Preston.

Carl Ikeme banner.

Finally, the support for Carl Ikeme throughout the season shows it's much more than a game.

The women's view

Jenny Wilkes, BBC WM presenter, president of the Official Wolves Supporters' Club and chair of Wolverhampton Wanderers Girls' and Women's Football Club, has gold and black running through her veins.

I'm a born and bred Wolves fan, attending the Golden Palace since the age of 10, and in that time I've seen plenty of highs and lows.

I was one of a handful of fans in the John Ireland Stand in 1986, watching Fourth Division football with Wolves playing on a pitch some distance from our stand – and with the Waterloo Road stand and North Bank both closed to the public.

I also remember interviewing manager Graham Turner in his office when he had a bucket in the corner to catch the drips from the leaky roof, and cockroaches running across the floor.

Jenny Wilkes.

Rúben Neves in short sleeves in mid-January.

We've come a long way since then, with great days at the Sherpa Van Trophy final at Wembley (when I had my hair dyed gold and black) and the Championship play-off win at the Millennium Stadium in Cardiff, but in all that time, I've never experienced a season like 2017-18.

When Nuno was appointed I think, like many fans, I was rather sceptical. Just like Walter Zenga, we hadn't heard of him and I didn't feel inspired by the appointment. Then came the Portuguese superstars we also didn't know, and I have to admit, rather like Steve Bruce, I was wondering how they'd fancy a chilly night game up north in January. As it turned out, Rúben Neves wore his short sleeves to take on the Beast from the East!

In contrast, Wolves Women weren't having a great season after an impressive promotion-winning campaign in 2016-17. In fact, Wolves Women often seem to be the antithesis of the men's side. As Walter Zenger and Paul Lambert's side were floundering, the women were fighting their way to the FA Women's Premier League, Midlands Division One title and promotion to the Northern Division.

Sadly, the higher level proved tricky, and the season didn't start well. After a change of manager just before Christmas, results started to improve, but despite winning the last game 5-0 and pushing Albion into the bottom spot, we still finished just above them in the relegation zone.

I've been chair of Wolves Girls and Women since 1999 when we were a separate self-financing entity. We've also had our highs and lows, but we're now very much part of the club, with the use of its training facilities and minibuses, and our Player of the Season honoured at the end-of-season dinner.

So back to the men, where we were putting in such gob-smacking performances that the very loud whinging old chap who sits just behind me in the Billy Quiet Stand had been struck dumb! In all my years following Wolves I've never before heard the crowd oooh-ing and aaah-ing at passes.

The most stressful game to watch for me was Middlesbrough away on March 30th, not helped by the fact that I was on holiday in Portugal. Along with three Wolves-supporting friends, I was driving back from the Algarve

Andrea Whetton with her Wolves Women's Player of the Season award.

and had left behind temperatures of 26 degrees, to find ourselves four hours later in Guarda in the north, in a snow storm!

We battled through the elements to find somewhere to watch the game but, after drawing a blank, we whipped out the trusty old laptop and settled down in a bar, with four of us hunched round the table, shouting and screaming. The Portuguese barman seemed to understand our predicament, and kept us topped up with beer and peanuts. To end up with nine players and defend our lead right to the very end was another demonstration of what an incredible team we have become.

As Nuno would say, it's a team effort. Obviously Neves takes the plaudits, but we couldn't have done it without the likes of Conor Coady and Matt Doherty who've been given a new lease of life. I've had plenty of Wolves heroes over the years – Dougan, Richards, Bull – but this is a team full of heroes.

So what about next season? Although the last time we were promoted I was full of optimism, this time I think my optimism will be justified. The feel-good factor's back in Wolverhampton and how far we've come from that empty stadium in 1986 to a packed Molineux with plans to expand to accommodate our ever-growing fan base.

There's plenty to look forward to from both Wolves men and women. Bring it on!

Daniel Harrison.

Returning to the fold

Daniel Harrison was a lapsed Wolves fan – until Nuno brought a new show to town.

Wolves supporters of a certain generation have developed an intuitive coping mechanism. Always expect the worst. Curb your enthusiasm. Anticipate the sting in the tail. Our suspicions heighten and fears worsen when a local rival comes to town but, on the evening of Saturday October 14th, 2017, things felt different.

There is a familiar rhetoric surrounding clashes with Aston Villa. The perennial chokers versus the former champions of Europe. The inferior outfit from the Black Country versus the big-city heavyweights.

Although Wolves had enjoyed recent successes in this fixture – a 1-0 home win under Paul Lambert the previous season and a Matt Jarvis-inspired victory at Villa Park in 2011 – Villa could point to disarray on their part or, perhaps, the quirks of derby day.

Not on this night. For the first time in years, those of gold and black persuasion had reason to approach the fixture with an air of superiority. There was a growing consensus that, for once, we had the measure of Villa in all departments. Better technicians. A more sophisticated brand of football. A shrewder tactician at the helm.

So it proved. On the most perfect of Saturday evenings – one which culminated in Wolves claiming top spot following Cardiff's draw with Birmingham 24 hours earlier – Nuno's men took the game to Villa with breath-taking panache and speed of thought. This was the moment that convinced me to re-join the Pack.

A supporter of three decades and a season ticket holder for much of that time, I'd suffered the lacklustre final few months of Colin Lee, the highs and lows of the Dave Jones era and the excruciating tenure of Glenn Hoddle, before lapsing at the end of Mick McCarthy's first season.

Admittedly, work reasons – a foray into sports journalism – were behind my hiatus, and when my career changed paths again a couple of years ago, the dour end to Kenny Jackett's reign and a chaotic start to the Fosun revolution gave me little appetite to reacquaint myself as a Molineux regular.

I've lived through four unsuccessful play-off campaigns, three relegations, an automatic promotion tilt under Graham Taylor that ended in glorious

Rúben Neves and Diogo Jota – eye-catching moments.

failure and another in 2001-02 which we no longer mention. Why would it be any different this time?

A first real glimpse of Nuno's Wolves quickly altered my mindset. In fact, it was evident a culture shift was sweeping through the whole club. Suddenly we had generation-defining players like Jota and Neves producing the most eye-catching football many of us have ever seen at Molineux, but it wasn't just the aesthetic. It was the relative ease and control with which this team carried itself throughout the campaign.

From the moment Nuno's side hit the front in one of European club football's most competitive leagues, there was little about their make-up to believe they wouldn't complete the job. If the swashbuckling Wolves of 2017-18 displayed, time after time, their ability to entertain us, those stunningly resilient away wins at Bristol City and Cardiff underpinned the culture shift that had taken hold. There would be no "choking" this time.

To an absent and much-loved friend

Wolves' former head of media Paul Berry pays tribute to his ex-colleague John 'Foz' Hendley who sadly passed away during the season.

Happier times – Foz (far right) with the Wolves media team.

I still remember the last time I saw Foz. It was nothing spectacular or out of the ordinary. It was just as he was leaving the office after my last working day at Wolves, a Saturday evening following the 1-0 win against Ipswich just before Christmas, 2017. We said our farewells, and vowed to meet up for a pint or two early in the New Year.

It was memorable because a few minutes earlier the whole media department had ventured into the lower tier of the Billy Wright Stand for a 'team photo' taken by Dave Bagnall, whom Foz had known for years. The photo showed three different generations of ages with Foz, the doyen of us all, smiling broadly. We are all so glad we have that photo to treasure his memory.

The previous day he had given a speech at the presentation to mark my departure from Wolves, after nine-and-a-half years' service, during which we had worked together through some great times, some run-of-the-mill times, and some seriously difficult times.

Anyone who worked with Foz during his two 'official' decades at Wolves will undoubtedly say that sometimes it was a challenge, but a wonderful challenge. He had his grumpy moments, particularly in a morning, but, when he was on song – a deliberate pun given his love of folk music and performing – his personality was infectious and he was great company.

Foz's love of Wolves was unconditional. He was brought up within sight of Molineux, his spiritual home, and from the moment – as a 15-year-old – he attended his first game at the behest of a fellow catering student from the Polytechnic, he was hooked.

It was a huge honour for Foz to eventually work for the club, firstly writing for the programme and website, and then, on a full-time basis as a press officer. For two decades he lived his dream, working day-in day-out with his heroes, from travelling up and down the country to watch his team, to being part of the pre-season tour – the full works!

A run of attending over 1,000 matches in succession made him particularly proud; that he would continue that sequence, including attending a match at Villa Park despite suffering from chickenpox at the time, came as no surprise to all who knew him.

In a way, amidst the terrible shock and sadness which greeted his sudden passing at the start of 2018, it was somehow fitting that his last home game was against Ipswich – when he shared an embrace and a chat with Mick McCarthy and Terry Connor whom he had so much respect for – and his last away trip at Bristol City, when Ryan Bennett's dramatic late winner continued Wolves' relentless pursuit of an ultimately fantastic, title-winning season.

Foz particularly cherished building those relationships with managers, backroom staff and players – in particular with the likes of Mick McCarthy and Dave Jones who built successful squads with characters, both in the dugout and the dressing room, with whom Foz so warmly identified. Whether it was going out for a curry with Vio Ganea, bantering with Bully, playing guitar on *Midlands Today* with Karl Henry, or, further in the past, golfing weekends with Mike Stowell and company, Foz loved his time working with the players, and they loved him in return.

So too did his Wolves colleagues, particularly Lorraine Hennessy and Catherine Preece with whom he shared the 2003 play-off triumph, as well as the Molineux media corps, including the author of this book, Dave Harrison. There was never a dull moment when Foz entered a press room, and it was only too fitting and a wonderful gesture from Wolves to name the new media suite for the 2018-19 Premier League in his honour.

Then there was the Albion. Oh blimey the Albion! For obvious and tribal reasons, Foz was not a fan. We never tired of his anecdote about the rather messy break-up with a former partner in which she fiercely declared: "You love the Wolves more than me." To be met, without fear or trepidation, with the swift retort: "I love the Albion more than you."

Yet, such were the magnificent contradictions contained within Foz's character, that some of the people he got on best with were of a Baggies' persuasion: his brother-in-law, Ray; Albion stalwarts John Homer and Dave Holloway, with whom he would travel the country taking in new stadia; former *Birmingham Mail* writers Chris Lepkowski and Bill Howell – Foz's matchday drinking partner; and his long-term singing partner and friend, John Richards, to name a few from a long list.

Even when Wolves Academy lined up against the old Black Country enemy, Foz would wait at the bottom of the steps as they went up to lunch the day before the game to wish them luck, and he'd be there again, the Monday morning after the game, either congratulating them on a famous win or chastising them for a poor result.

That was Foz. He had the extraordinary ability to be able to interact with people of all ages and all backgrounds. As the years passed, and despite the age gap between him and his colleagues growing wider, he remained hugely popular. A poignant illustration of this was that, among so many former Wolves players who attended his memorial service, the two among the current squad – Danny Batth and Harry Burgoyne – had themselves come through the ranks and would have seen Foz every day around the club.

The Wolves media department, as seen on that photo, spanned the generations, and while the ever-changing media landscape did lead to some challenges in the office, boy, were there some laughs. At times, with Foz's delivery of a particular story or historical anecdote, the laughter was so strong that it almost turned into tears.

On January 2nd, 2018, the tears were for an altogether different reason.

Danny Batth and former defender Kevin Foley with a floral tribute for Foz.

Wolves players pay tribute to Foz before the FA Cup game against Swansea.

While there are many regrets that we never did get to have that pint or two and continue our 15-year friendship, which preceded our time as colleagues, there are so many memories, conversations and typical 'Foz-isms' which will always raise a smile. His influence will never be far away.

There were so many people who will have undoubtedly been thinking about Foz on the day Wolves clinched promotion after such a fantastic season, or the day the title was sealed at Bolton, the trophy lift against Sheffield Wednesday, the Bank Holiday parade. He was missed everywhere.

His love of Wolves, knowledge of the club's history, interaction over so many years with so many people involved with the club, and, above all his unique personality, will certainly ensure that Foz will never ever be forgotten.

An author's verdict

Steve Gordos, who has written several books on Wolves, casts his author's expert eye on the team that Nuno built.

I have to be honest. I was far from optimistic about the 2017-18 season. We had a new manager I had not heard of and he was a goalkeeper, like one of his unsuccessful predecessors. I do not rate goalkeepers as football coaches.

Steve Gordos.

We also had several new players whose ability to cope with the demands of the Championship was anyone's guess. Their names were not familiar. Rúben Neves sounded like a mountain in Scotland.

I voiced my doubts to anyone who would listen and am happy to say I got it totally wrong. My fears were groundless. Manager Nuno got the team playing a brand of football I cannot recall seeing in 64 years of watching Wolves. No Wolves team in my years have possessed so many gifted players capable of individual brilliance. Neves, Hélder Costa, Diogo Jota and Ivan Cavaleiro are men who can conjure up moments of magic.

Stan Cullis' superb side of the 1950s likewise managed excitement and goals but played a direct style of football. Nuno's team, however, prefer a studied approach which can suddenly erupt into glorious attacking thrusts. They have taken Wolves football to a new level of excellence.

Some of the skills exhibited by the current Wolves players can compare to those of the great Peter Broadbent. I can offer no greater compliment. He was probably the most naturally gifted player I have seen in a gold shirt, closely followed by Peter Knowles.

Over the years I have seen many other Wolves players who could turn a match on their own – Johnny Hancocks, Jimmy Mullen, Dennis Wilshaw, John Richards, Dave Wagstaffe and Steve Bull being among them – but the present squad have produced goals and drama to rank alongside the achievements of those who before them wore the gold shirt with distinction.

The win at Bristol City with ten men, the rearguard action with nine to win at Middlesbrough and the unbelievable climax to the game at Cardiff with its two missed penalties – these games will be talked about for years to come, just as my generation recall the wins over Honvéd, Spartak and Real Madrid.

I have seen great goals with power shooting from the likes of Ron Flowers, Terry Wharton, Alan Hinton and Steve Bull but I have never seen a better goal than the one Neves scored against Derby. Likewise, I can remember attacking full-backs like Gerry Harris and Bobby Thomson but never two in the same team as we have with Barry Douglas and Matt Doherty. I can also recall cool calm central defenders like Billy Wright, Bill Slater and Frank Munro. The displays by Conor Coady and Willy Boly this season have put me in mind of those Molineux legends.

Those of us old enough to have seen Wolves in the 1950s and 1970s probably thought we would never see their like again. That was a view I held years ago but I was so much older then, I'm younger than that now, thanks to the team that Nuno built.

From behind the lens

Photographer Dave Bagnall offers a pitch side view of the title-winning season and how Nuno's team recaptured his interest.

I started photographing Wolves matches just under 40 years ago and it got off to a good start, beating Forest at Wembley and two FA Cup semi-finals in the first few years, but towards the end of last season I was thinking of packing it in because I was starting to get bored with the style of football I was photographing.

When I heard we had appointed a new manager called Nuno Espírito Santo my first thought was, what a great name but who is he and what's he done? Then I found he was a former goalkeeper and thought that's not going to work – goalies don't make good managers – but,

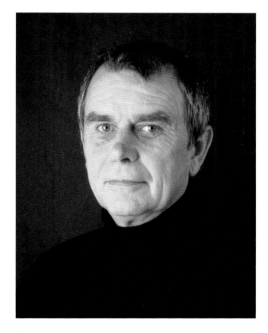

for some reason, I didn't stop taking the photographs and what I have seen this season is the best football I have ever seen at Molineux.

Working on the touchline next to the goals I am sandwiched between the players and the fans and, over the years, I have heard some tasty language and groans when things weren't going well on the pitch but this season has been like no other season I can remember.

For the first time ever I have found myself joining with the singing *Nuno had a Dream* and then I can't get the songs out of my head for days after. The only angry voices this season have all been aimed at the referee and his assistants, while the famous chant 'You don't know what you're doing' has been reserved just for the officials.

Dave Bagnall.

Even when we dropped points or even lost at home I have been amazed how positive the supporters have been. There appears to be a very special bond between the manager, players and fans, especially with the fans and Nuno, as I can't ever remember supporters being more excited about meeting the manager than the players. The love is mutual because Nuno appears to adore the Wolves fans as much as they do him, and during the recent celebrations he was orchestrating the supporters himself.

When Steve Bruce suggested we might struggle through the long winter months I assumed he was referring to our continental players not fancying it on a cold winter's night. I remember thinking Bruce might have a valid point until I was leaving Molineux after a night match at Molineux in early winter. It was freezing cold as I was struggling up the hill to the car park with all my camera gear. Half way up the hill I stopped and behind me was a tough looking guy wearing shorts and his name was Rúben Neves. I got the impression that a bit of cold weather wasn't going to bother him one bit.

Part of my work involves photographing the players with the match day mascots and the junior Wolves fans parties. All I can say is that every member of the team has been absolutely fantastic with their interaction with the kids and their parents. Their attitude is spot-on and a pleasure to see. It's always 'high fives' with all the kids they meet and they never refuse a 'selfie' with anyone. I think it's safe to say we don't have any 'Big Time Charlies' in our team.

Just before kick-off for the home game against Forest I had a chat with Robert Plant and we both laughed that the season had been like a dream that we were scared we might wake up from, then Forest woke us up by winning 2-0. Thankfully, we were soon back in dreamland, winning three on the trot.

Robert Plant living the dream with Hélder Costa.

Tears turn to cheers

Dan Warren watched the sleeping giant awake and take the Championship by storm.

What a season to be a Wolves fan! I fully expect to be talking about this team in 30 to 40 years' time. As a fan whose earliest memory was the play-off final in 2003, I haven't had a great deal to cheer about and certainly had a lot to cry about.

I haven't had the experience of watching the great teams of the '40s, '50s and '70s (except on *YouTube*). The nearest was the 2008-09 season when Mick McCarthy took us up as champions, but we were nowhere near as good a side.

I had mixed feelings going into the season. I was concerned at the way Paul Lambert and Kenny Jackett had been sacked in Fosun's first season in charge (not to mention the Zenga experiment). However, I had a feeling that the club was starting to get it right with the appointment of Nuno and his transformation of the squad. There were also signs of the new club management reconnecting with the fans with reduced season ticket prices and attractive incentives.

The summer signings of Jota, Neves, Boly and Bonatini really excited me. Of course, there were the critics who said "All these foreign players, how will they cope at Millwall and Barnsley in midweek?" So I've enjoyed singing the song *Shit in the Winter* every time we caned a team in midweek at very cold temperatures.

Dan Warren.

There are games that stick out for me, throughout the course of the season, that made me think this season was going to be special. Firstly, the opening game against Middlesbrough, the early favourites to win the league, when we saw a calm and controlled performance by Wolves. We dominated them and picked them off on the counter attack.

Three wins from the opening four games made a statement and I arrived at Griffin Park for the Brentford game to hear that the chairman Jeff Shi and managing director Laurie Dalrymple were buying Wolves fans shots in a local pub. By now there was a feeling of what Nuno called the pack mentality with chairman, manager, players and fans united – something that hadn't happened for years.

Even though the Brentford game ended 0-0 it showed that Wolves could win points ugly. The stand-out performers at this game were Boly and Coady, the latter being my player of the season as his conversion to sweeper was a master stroke by Nuno.

Another stand-out game for me was Middlesbrough away on Good Friday. I had travelled up to Teesside on a Bank Holiday for four hours in awful traffic. I have to say I've never shouted so much at a game. Wolves were cruising 2-0

Barry Douglas and his wife Debbie.
(AMA Sports Photo Agency)

at half time, only to be down to nine men by the 65th minute and holding on. It was a rollercoaster of emotion.

Coady and Boly again were masterful, throwing themselves at every cross and shot Boro hurled at us. Nuno and the fans were heading every ball away and the celebrations at the end of that game gave me the belief that nothing was stopping this team!

Rúben Neves is the best player I have ever seen in a Wolves shirt. His diagonal balls, feeding Cavaleiro and Jota and the wing backs Doherty and Douglas have simply devastated opposing sides. His importance, defensively, showed when he was suspended for the Fulham game, the only time all season that Wolves were played off the park.

In all it was a great season with much to look forward to in the Premier League, I believe the sleeping giant of English football is awakening.

A united pack of Fosun, Uncle Jorge Mendes, Nuno, the players and the fans is a prospect that will shake the Premier League. Man City, we are coming for you!

The Generation Game

The Butler family, grandfather Tony, father Ross and son Joseph, aged nine, have revelled in the shared experience of watching their team.

Tony Butler

I started going to Wolves matches in 1962, with my dad Ray, when I was 10 years old, and the first game I watched was a floodlit evening match against Aston Villa that ended goalless. To me, the players were awe inspiring and so quick. Wolves had a good team then.

As I got older I played Sunday league football and we got to the JW Hunt Cup final, which should have been played at Molineux but wasn't that year due to the John Ireland stand being built. So when the opportunity came along to play at Molineux before Mike Stowell's testimonial I jumped at the chance.

It is one of my best memories, playing in the match with the likes of Steve Daly, Keith Downing, Mel Eves and Phil Parkes amongst others. We won 3-2 which was great and a real dream come true to play on hallowed ground.

Moving onto today's team with Nuno, it is a world apart from back in my childhood. This is the best football I have ever seen played at Molineux. There is a real feeling of excitement in the atmosphere and the quality of the players are amazing.

My favourite goal of this season was Neves' goal against Derby. Pre-Rúben, it was one of the goals in Derek Dougan's hat-trick on his debut against Hull, and highlights the different class of football being played between in different eras.

Ross Butler

I have always loved the Wolves and for many years, when I was much younger, me and my dad had season tickets. I have many fond memories of Wolves in the old fourth, third and second divisions, standing on the South Bank poised to jump into a walkway when we scored so as not to be crushed!

This season I got my son, Joseph, a season ticket as he had begun to take an interest in football. Joseph now believes that this has always been Wolves' style of football!

Portuguese perfection - Nuno celebrating with his family at Molineux. (AMA Sports Photo Agency)

Joseph Butler.

Returning regularly to Molineux over the course of the season I have witnessed a very well organised club from top to bottom. Sir Jack Hayward was fantastic but never had the right people around him to deliver his vision. The expectation now is the same as in the 1990s but the energy around the club is so much more positive compared with back then.

Nuno has assembled a team oozing quality which has been spectacular to watch, to the point where, at first, people thought I was exaggerating the style of football Wolves were playing. During a discussion with a Manchester United fan, I advised him Wolves were more entertaining than them – the first time I've ever been able to say that and mean it!

We applauded the players, Nuno and the staff at every game, and they too have shown appreciation for the fans. The rapport between the club and fans is unlike anything I have seen here.

The whole season was an experience that both Joseph and I will always remember.

Joseph Butler

I have loved going to the football with Dad. I have been able to learn lots about the game and have really started to enjoy playing it too. I love sitting in the stand listening to the music booming around, and everyone coming in excited to see Wolves play and win another match. My favourite song is *Nuno had a Dream*.

There have been so many good players this season it's been really hard to pick an absolute favourite but the goal Neves scored against Derby will always be one of the best goals I remember most.

I also love that this is something I get to do with my dad!

From behind the microphone

BBC WM commentator Daz Hale managed to keep his emotions in check – until that day in Cardiff.

Daz Hale.

I've been covering football for BBC WM since 2002 and have always felt absolutely privileged to be able to do so, even more so when it involves my beloved Wolverhampton Wanderers.

I've been a season ticket holder at Molineux for most of my life and even after all of these years, I still get butterflies and that 'matchday tingle' every time I make my way down Waterloo Road to see 'me babbies' in action.

One question I'm often asked about being on the radio is how I manage to keep my emotions (relatively!) in check when behind the microphone, and not behave as I would with my mates on the South Bank. My stock answer has always been that, like Worzel Gummidge, I have a different head on. So, when on official duty, I am mindful of that fact that I am a professional broadcaster representing the BBC.

It's not a hobby, it's my job, my career, my livelihood. When I'm 'at work', I have a responsibility to my employers, the listeners, and myself to behave and carry myself in such a manner which reflects the position I hold.

All of which sounds good in theory and, for the most part, it has worked in practice too. That was until Friday, April 6 at approximately 9.35pm. It was the moment when, for a few seconds, I genuinely forgot I was on air and found myself bear-hugging Mel Eves in the press box at Cardiff, while screaming like a teenage girl at a One Direction concert.

There were crazy scenes on the pitch and in the commentary box at the Cardiff City Stadium.

Graham Large.

Ivan Cavaleiro dances round defenders.

All this after the home side incredibly missed those two stoppage time penalties to all but hand Wolves promotion and the Championship title. Yep, I lost it and, looking around, I wasn't the only one of my media colleagues to do so either. It was carnage in Cardiff!

Thinking about it, there must be something in the air at the Welsh capital which brings out the extreme emotions in me. Fifteen years earlier I'd shed a tear in the same city, down the road at the Millennium Stadium, after the boys in gold and black beat another Neil Warnock side (Sheffield United) to clinch their first promotion to the Premier League.

However, this promotion to the top division feels different from that, and the other in 2009 when the team spent most of their time just swimming against the tide of relegation. This time there is a genuine belief that Wolves are entering a golden new era.

Will Nuno's dream stop the yo-yo-ing up and down the leagues? I hope so, as I can once again try to revert to being the consummate pro in the press box. I'm sure Mel Eves' eardrums hope so too!

Excitement and pride

Writer and fanzine editor Graham Large relives the moments when Wolves erased their history of underachievement.

When the Wanderers win, we know how to party.

That statement was no less true than after a 0-0 draw against Sheffield Wednesday in the final home game of the season, when the streets of Wolverhampton were awash with

Time to celebrate.

Wanderers fans making the most of their side's glory. About 8,000 of us woke up early and congregated around Molineux nearly three hours before kick-off and, when the full-time whistle sounded, there was absolute chaos. Who would normally celebrate a 'bore draw' with such vigour?

Even now it seems hard to fathom, not least the sensational manner in which Wolves won promotion to the top flight of English football, but just what a season it was and how we became champions. No one quite knew what to expect when the relatively unheard of Nuno Espírito Santo arrived, but within a few weeks he not only changed the club's tactics, formation, and methods but he signed 12 new players and completely rejuvenated a club that had been underachieving since relegation from the top flight in 2012.

I could say it was a campaign that had it all: twists and turns, ups and downs, unpredictability and world-class talent but, apart from the latter, this was far from the usual rollercoaster ride as Wolves hit the ground running with three consecutive victories and from late October onwards they remained rooted to top spot, winning promotion with four games to spare.

The world-class talent I mentioned is one Rúben Neves who, when playing for Porto, was the youngest ever captain to play in the Champions League. He was easily the best player in the Championship during the season and one that many Wolves fans have called the best to ever grace the turf at Molineux.

Nuno and the players show their appreciation to the fans.

However, the pleasing thing about this season is it's been a team effort. Diogo Jota has been a constant threat. Willy Boly has been a mountain in defence. Ivan Cavaleiro has danced around defenders, and Conor Coady has led the line like a true warrior. Every player has given his all.

Such a far cry from the days of Walter Zenga and Paul Lambert, when I started to question whether or not Fosun were truly committed to taking Wolves forward. Fortunately, those worries have been firmly laid to rest.

As for what happens next, I really don't know, but for the first time in a long time I'm excited and extremely proud to be a Wolves fan.

The 2017-18 Season Statistics
(compiled by Steve Gordos)

Appendix 1 – Championship

The man with a plan – it was Nuno's dream season.

Championship – August 5, 2017	
Wolves 1 Bonatini 33	Ruddy; Miranda, Coady, Boly, Doherty, Saïss, Neves, Douglas, Enobakhare (Edwards 78), Jota (Graham 84), Bonatini (Dicko 57). **Subs (unused):** Norris, Bennett, Batth, Ronan. **Booked:** Miranda 28
Middlesborough 0	Randolph; Christie, Ayala, Gibson, Friend, Howson (Gestede 81), Clayton, Braithwaite, de Roon (Forshaw 65), Assombalonga, Fletcher (Bamford 57). **Subs (unused):** Konstantopoulos, Fabio, Leadbitter, Fry. **Booked:** Clayton 58, Forshaw 90.

Attendance: 29,692	Top Six	Pld	Pts
	Bristol City	1	3
	Queens Park Rangers	1	3
	Cardiff City	1	3
	Ipswich Town	1	3
Referee:	Nottingham Forest	1	3
Darren Bond	Preston North End	1	3

Championship – August 12, 2017	
Derby County 0	Carson; Wisdom, Keogh, Davies, Forsyth, Butterfield (Bryson 63), Huddlestone, Johnson, Russell (Nugent 62), Martin, Weimann (Anya 71). **Subs (unused):** Mitchell, Baird, Pearce, Bennett.
Wolves 2 Douglas 32 Cavaleiro 76	Ruddy; Miranda, Coady, Boly, Doherty, Saïss, Neves, Douglas, Enobakhare (Ronan 81), Bonatini (Cavaleiro 65), Jota (Dicko 86). **Subs (unused):** Bennett, Batth, Price, Norris.

Attendance: 27,757	Top Six	Pld	Pts
	Cardiff City	2	6
	Wolves	2	6
	Nottingham Forest	2	6
	Ipswich Town	2	6
Referee:	Hull City	2	4
Lee Probert	Queens Park Rangers	2	4

Championship – August 15, 2017

Hull City 2 Dawson 27 Meyler 90+10 (pen)	McGregor; Aina, Dawson, Hector, Clark, Bowen (Larsson 60), Henriksen, Clucas, Grosicki, Hernandez (Meyler 86), Campbell (Diomande 76). **Subs (unused)**: Mannion, Mazuch, Weir, Lenihan. **Booked:** Campbell 70, Dawson 90.
Wolves 3 Neves 6 Jota 43 Dicko 90	Ruddy; Miranda, Coady, Boly, Doherty, Saïss, Neves, Douglas, Enobakhare (Cavaleiro 60), Bonatini (Dicko 75), Jota (Bennett 85). **Subs (unused)**: Norris, Batth, Graham, Price. Booked: Saïss 48, Jota 54, Neves 68, Cavaleiro 90

Attendance: 17,145	Top Six	Pld	Pts
	Cardiff City	3	9
	Wolves	3	9
	Ipswich Town	3	9
	Middlesbrough	3	6
Referee: Jeremy Simpson	Nottingham Forest	3	6
	Leeds United	3	5

Championship – August 19, 2017

Wolves 1 Bonatini 67	Ruddy; Miranda, Coady, Boly, Doherty, Saïss (Ronan 83), Neves, Douglas (Dicko 78), Enobakhare (Cavaleiro 58), Bonatini, Jota. **Subs (unused)**: Bennett, Batth, Price, Norris. **Booked:** Saïss 28, Douglas 61.
Cardiff City 2 Ralls 54 Mendez-Lang 77	Etheridge; Peltier, Morrison, Bamba, Richards, Gunnarsson, Ralls, Mendez-Lang, Damour (Ecuele Manga 90), Hoilett (Ward 83), Zohore. **Subs not used:** Murphy, Tomlin, Halford, Kennedy, Bogle. **Booked:** Hoilett 19, Ralls 38, Damour 45, Peltier 56

Attendance: 27,068	Top Six	Pld	Pts
	Cardiff City	4	12
	Ipswich Town	4	12
	Wolves	4	9
	Nottingham Forest	4	9
Referee: Scott Duncan	Leeds United	4	8
	Queens Park Rangers	4	7

Championship – August 26, 2017			
Brentford 0	Bentley; Dalsgaard, Dean, Barbet (Bjelland 72), Colin, Mokotjo (Woods 65), Yennaris, Jota (Jozefzoon 65), Sawyers, Watkins, Murphy. **Subs (unused)**: Egan, Clarke, Daniels, Canos. **Booked:** Dean 36		
Wolves 0	Ruddy; Miranda, Coady, Boly, Doherty, Saïss, Neves (Price 86), Vinagre, Enobakhare (Cavaleiro HT), Bonatini (Dicko 78), Jota. **Subs (unused)**: Bennett, Batth, Ronan, Norris. **Booked:** Doherty 43.		
Attendance: 10,351	**Top Six**	**Pld**	**Pts**
	Cardiff City	5	15
	Ipswich Town	5	12
	Leeds United	5	11
	Wolves	5	10
Referee:	Sheffield United	5	9
Tim Robinson	Nottingham Forest	5	9

Championship – September 9, 2017			
Wolves 1 Jota 10	Ruddy; Batth, Coady, Miranda, Doherty, Saiss, Neves (N'Diaye 77), Vinagre, Marshall (Enobakhare 59), Bonatini, Jota (Cavaleiro 87**)**. **Subs (unused):** Price, Ronan, Norris, Deslandes. **Booked:** Batth 57.		
Millwall 0	Archer; McLaughlin, Webster, Hutchinson, Meredith (Ferguson 79), Wallace (Onyedinma 79), Williams, Saville, O'Brien, Morison, Gregory. **Subs (unused):** King, Craig, Romeo, Tunnicliffe, Cooper. **Booked:** Webster 41. **Sent off:** O'Brien 65		
Attendance: 24,426	**Top Six**	**Pld**	**Pts**
	Cardiff City	6	16
	Leeds United	6	14
	Wolves	6	13
	Ipswich Town	6	12
Referee:	Sheffield United	6	12
Robert Madley	Middlesbrough	6	10

Championship – September 12, 2017	
Wolves 3 Bonatini 28 Jota 54 Batth 85	Ruddy; Batth, Coady, Miranda (Saïss 76), Doherty, N'Diaye, Neves (Marshall 84), Vinagre, Cavaleiro (Enobakhare 76), Bonatini, Jota. **Subs (unused)**: Zyro, Price, Norris, Deslandes. **Booked:** Jota 68.
Bristol City 3 Flint 43 Diedhiou 58 (pen) Reid 82	Fielding; Wright, Flint, Baker, Bryan, O'Dowda, Smith, Brownhill (Paterson 77), Leko (Taylor 68), Diedhiou (Pack 78), Reid. **Subs (unused):** Steele, Woodrow, Eliasson, Magnusson. **Booked:** Baker 21, Brownhill 48.

Attendance: 23,045	Top Six	Pld	Pts
	Leeds United	7	17
	Cardiff City	7	16
	Sheffield United	7	15
	Wolves	7	14
Referee:	Preston North End	7	12
Steve Martin	Sheffield Wednesday	7	12

Diogo Jota celebrates with Alfred N'Diaye after scoring against Bristol City.

Championship – September 16, 2017	
Nottm Forest 1 Carayol 75	Smith; Darikwa, Worrall, Mills, Traore, Bridcutt, Osborn, Brereton (Walker 86), Dowell (Carayol 62), McKay (Cummings 71), Murphy. **Subs (unused):** Henderson, Lichaj, Fox, Bouchalakis. **Booked:** Mills 82, Bridcutt 90+3.
Wolves 2 Jota 47, 81	Ruddy; Batth, Coady, Miranda, Doherty, Saïss, Neves, Vinagre (Deslandes 64), Cavaleiro (Marshall 62), Bonatini (N'Diaye 83), Jota. **Subs (unused):** Price, Ronan, Enobakhare, Norris. **Booked:** Cavaleiro 56, Marshall 90.

Attendance: 25,756	Top Six	Pld	Pts
	Leeds United	8	17
	Wolves	8	17
	Cardiff City	8	17
	Preston North End	8	15
Referee:	Ipswich Town	7	15
Geoff Eltringham	Sheffield United	8	15

Championship – September 23, 2017	
Wolves 2 Enobakhare 80 N'Diaye 90+3	Ruddy; Batth, Coady, Miranda, Doherty, Saïss (N'Diaye 80), Neves, Vinagre (Douglas HT), Cavaleiro (Enobakhare 65), Bonatini, Jota. **Subs (unused):** Norris, Marshall, Costa, Price. Booked: Neves 47, Coady 57, Saïss 70.
Barnsley 1 Jackson 90+1	Davies; McCarthy, Jackson, Lindsay, Pearson, Williams, Hammill, Moncur (McGeehan 82), Potts (Ugbo 82), Barnes (Hedges 70), Bradshaw. **Subs (unused):** Townsend, MacDonald, Pinnock, Thiam. **Booked:** Williams 27

Attendance: 28,154	Top Six	Pld	Pts
	Leeds United	9	20
	Wolves	9	20
	Cardiff City	9	20
	Preston North End	9	16
Referee:	Middlesbrough	9	15
Jeremy Simpson	Ipswich Town	8	15

Championship – September 27, 2017	
Sheffield United 2 Clarke 39 58	Blackman; Carter-Vickers, Wright (Duffy 56), O'Connell, Baldock, Basham, Coutts, Fleck, Stevens (Lafferty HT), Brooks, Clarke (Evans 79). **Subs (unused)**: Moore, Lundstram, Sharp, Carruthers. **Booked**: Coutts 54, Basham 67, Baldock 75.
Wolves 0	Ruddy; Batth, Coady, Miranda, Doherty, N'Diaye, Neves (Cavaleiro 64), Douglas, Costa (Saïss 20), Bonatini (Enobakhare HT), Jota. **Subs (unused)**: Norris, Marshall, Price, Vinagre. **Sent off**: Coady 15. **Booked**: Neves 61

Attendance: 25,893	Top Six	Pld	Pts
	Cardiff City	10	23
	Sheffield United	10	21
	Leeds United	10	20
	Wolves	10	20
Referee:	Preston North End	10	19
Peter Bankes	Ipswich Town	9	18

Championship – September 30, 2017	
Burton Albion 0	Bywater; Buxton, McFadzean, Warnock, Flanagan (Naylor HT), Akpan (Sordell 58), Murphy, Allen, Dyer, Atkins, Scannell (Varney 67). **Subs (unused)**: Lund, Ripley, Palmer, Barker. **Booked**: Varney 78.
Wolves 4 Jota 5 Saïss 11 Vinagre 41 Bonatini 62.	Ruddy; Bennett, Batth, Miranda, Doherty, Neves (Price 74), Saïss, Vinagre, Costa (Bonatini 51), Jota (Ronan 77), Cavaleiro. **Subs (unused)**: Norris, N'Diaye, Enobakhare, Deslandes

Attendance: 5,080	Top Six	Pld	Pts
	Cardiff City	11	24
	Wolves	11	23
	Sheffield United	11	21
	Leeds United	10	20
Referee:	Bristol City	11	20
Tony Harrington	Preston North End	11	20

Championship – October 14, 2017	
Wolves 2 Jota 55 Bonatini 71	Ruddy; Batth, Coady, Miranda, Doherty, Saïss, Neves (N'Diaye 79), Douglas, Costa (Bonatini HT), Cavaleiro (Marshall 73), Jota. **Subs (unused)**: Norris, Bennett, Enobakhare, Vinagre.
Aston Villa 0	Johnstone; El Mohamady, Chester, Terry, Hutton, Snodgrass, Whelan, Hourihane, Adomah (Onomah 73), Kodja (O'Hare 79), Davis (Hogan 64). **Subs (unused)**: Steer, de Laet, Samba, Bjarnason. **Booked:** Snodgrass 12, Hourihane 42.

Attendance: 30,239	**Top Six**	**Pld**	**Pts**
	Wolves	12	26
	Cardiff	12	24
	Sheffield United	12	24
	Bristol City	12	21
Referee:	Preston North End	12	21
Andy Davies	Leeds United	12	20

Game over! Léo Bonatini scores as Wolves go 2-0 up against Villa.

Championship – October 21, 2017	
Wolves 3 Cavaleiro 44 Bonatini 59 (pen), 63.	Ruddy; Batth, Coady, Miranda, Doherty, Saïss, Neves, Douglas, Cavaleiro (Enobakhare 75), Bonatini (Costa 75), Jota (N'Diaye 83). **Subs (unused):** Norris, Bennett, Marshall, Price. **Booked:** Douglas 73, Miranda 85, Saiss 90.
Preston NE 2 Hugill 65 Coady (og) 76	Maxwell; Fisher, Huntington, Davies, Earl, Pearson, Johnson, Barkhuizen, Browne, Harrop (Mavididi 61), Hugill. **Subs (unused):** Hudson, Boyle, Horgan, Gallagher, Woods, Robinson. **Booked:** Huntington 71, Johnson 90, Hugill 90. **Sent off:** Browne 90+1.

	Top Six	Pld	Pts
Attendance: 27,352	Wolves	13	29
	Cardiff	13	27
	Sheffield United	13	27
	Leeds United	13	23
Referee:	Aston Villa	13	22
Steve Martin	Bristol City	13	21

Championship – October 28, 2017	
QPR 2 Washington 41 Smith 81	Smithies; Baptiste, Lynch, Robinson, Cousins (Wszolek 66), Luongo, Scowen, Freeman (Furlong 90+2), Bidwell, Sylla (Smith 66), Washington. **Subs (unused):** Mackie, N'Gbakoto, Lumley, Wheeler. **Booked:** Bidwell 45, Cousins 60, Luongo 79, Lynch 90.
Wolves 1 Bonatini 43	Ruddy; Batth, Coady, Miranda, Doherty, Saïss, Neves (Marshall 84), Douglas, Cavaleiro (Costa 57), Bonatini (Enobakhare 71), Jota. **Subs (unused):** Norris, N'Diaye, Bennett, Boly. **Booked:** Saïss 90

	Top Six	Pld	Pts
Attendance: 16,004	Sheffield United	14	30
	Wolves	14	29
	Cardiff City	14	28
	Bristol City	14	24
Referee:	Leeds United	14	23
Tony Harrington	Aston Villa	13	22

Championship – October 31, 2017	
Norwich City 0	Gunn; Pinto, Hanley, Klose, Husband (Stiepermann 60), Reed, Trybull (Zimmermann 65), Vrancic, Maddison, Murphy (Jerome 60), Watkins. **Subs (unused)**: McGovern, Martin, Hoolahan, Cantwell. **Booked**: Watkins 29, Murphy 53, Stiepermann 90, Reed 90.
Wolves 2 Boly 18 Bonatini 72	Ruddy; Bennett, Coady, Boly, Doherty, N'Diaye, Neves, Douglas, Cavaleiro (Enobakhare 61), Bonatini (Price 76), Jota (Costa 84). **Subs (unused)**: Norris, Marshall, Vinagre, Hause. **Booked**: Cavaleiro 41, Neves 64, Douglas 73, Bennett 80.

Attendance: 26,554	**Top Six**	**Pld**	**Pts**
	Wolves	15	32
	Cardiff City	15	31
	Sheffield United	15	30
	Bristol City	15	27
Referee:	Derby County	14	25
Darren England	Leeds United	15	23

Championship – November 3, 2017	
Wolves 2 Saïss 9 Bonatini 26	Ruddy; Bennett, Coady, Boly (N'Diaye 79), Doherty, Saïss, Neves, Douglas, Cavaleiro (Enobakhare 75), Bonatini (Marshall 87), Jota. **Subs (unused)**: Norris, Batth, Costa, Vinagre. **Booked**: Saiss 42, Douglas 53.
Fulham 0	Button; Fredericks, Odoi, Ream, Ryan Sessegnon, Norwood, McDonald, Johansen, Ayite (Soares Alves 63), Fonte (Kamara 70), Kebano (Mollo 54). **Subs (unused)**: Bettinelli, Kalas, Edun, Cisse. **Booked**: Johansen 1, Norwood 13, Sessegnon 25, McDonald 49.

Attendance: 24,388	**Top Six**	**Pld**	**Pts**
	Wolves	16	35
	Cardiff City	15	31
	Sheffield United	15	30
	Bristol City	15	27
Referee:	Aston Villa	15	26
David Coote	Derby County	14	25

Championship – November 18, 2017	
Reading 0	Mannone; McShane, Ilori (Edwards 31), Moore, Bacuna, Van den Berg, Swift, Gunter, Beerens (Bodvarsson 81), Kermorgant (Aluko 66), Barrow. **Subs (unused)**: Jaakkola, Clement, Blackett, Richards. **Booked**: Bacuna 20, van den Berg 56.
Wolves 2 Cavaleiro 16 Doherty 88	Ruddy; Bennett, Coady, Boly, Doherty, Saïss, Neves, Vinagre, Cavaleiro (N'Diaye 79), Bonatini (Enobakhare 72), Jota (Costa 85). **Subs (unused)**: Norris, Batth, Price, Miranda. **Booked**: Doherty 59, Bennett 64.

Attendance: 20,708	Top Six	Pld	Pts
	Wolves	17	38
	Sheffield United	17	36
	Cardiff City	17	34
	Bristol City	17	31
Referee:	Aston Villa	17	29
Roger East	Middlesbrough	16	26

Championship – November 22, 2017	
Wolves 4 Douglas 15 Cavaleiro 26 Jota 72 Costa 76 (pen)	Ruddy; Bennett, Coady, Boly, Doherty, Saïss (N'Diaye 81), Neves (Price 80), Douglas, Cavaleiro (Costa 69), Bonatini, Jota. **Subs (unused)**: Norris, Batth, Miranda, Enobakhare.
Leeds United 1 Alioski 48	Lonergan; Ayling, Jansson, Cooper, Berardi, Vieira, Phillips, Alioski, Saiz (Dallas 77), Hernandez (O'Kane 69), Roofe (Ekuban 69). **Subs (unused)**: Wiedwald, Pennington, Anita, Shaughnessy. **Booked**: Phillips 51, Alioski 62. **Sent off**: Vieira 60.

Attendance: 28,914	Top Six	Pld	Pts
	Wolves	18	41
	Cardiff City	18	37
	Sheffield United	18	36
	Aston Villa	18	32
Referee:	Bristol City	18	31
Geoff Eltringham	Middlesbrough	18	29

Championship – November 25, 2017	
Wolves 5 Boly 13 Bonatini 25, Cavaleiro 62 (pen), 82 Jota 87.	Ruddy; Bennett, Coady, Boly, Doherty, Saïss, Neves, Douglas (Vinagre 89), Cavaleiro (N'Diaye 85), Bonatini (Costa 72), Jota. **Subs (unused)**: Norris, Batth, Price, Enobakhare. **Booked**: Jota 58, Neves 64.
Bolton W. 1 Buckley 74.	Alnwick; Little, Wheater, Beevers, Robinson, Pratley (Le Fondre 78), Henry, Ameobi (Noone 63), Vela, Armstrong (Buckley 63), Madine. **Subs (unused)**: Howard, Cullen, Darby, Burke. Wheater 43, Ameobi 45

Attendance: 27,894	Top Six	Pld	Pts
	Wolves	19	44
	Cardiff City	18	37
	Sheffield United	19	37
	Aston Villa	19	35
Referee:	Bristol City	19	34
Keith Stroud	Derby County	19	32

Ivan Cavaleiro scores to make it 3-0 to Wolves.

Championship – December 4, 2017	
Birmingham City 0	Stockdale; Roberts, Morrison, Dean, Nsue, Kieftenbeld, Ndoye (Davis 80), Grounds, Boga, Jutkiewicz (Adams 68), Jota (Gleeson HT). **Subs (unused)**: Trueman, Gallagher, Maghoma, Cotterill. **Booked**: Roberts 12, Morrison 83. **Sent off**: Dean 83.
Wolves 1 Bonatini 8	Ruddy; Bennett, Coady, Boly, Doherty, Saïss (Enobakhare 80), N'Diaye, Douglas, Cavaleiro (Costa 61), Bonatini (Price 65), Jota. **Subs (unused)**: Norris, Batth, Miranda, Vinagre. **Booked**: N'Diaye 67, Jota 83.

Attendance: 19,641	Top Six	Pld	Pts
	Wolves	20	47
	Cardiff City	20	43
	Bristol City	20	37
	Sheffield United	20	37
Referee:	Aston Villa	20	36
Simon Hooper	Derby County	20	15

Léo Bonatini celebrates with his teammates after putting Wolves 1-0 ahead.

Championship – December 9, 2017	
Wolves 0	Ruddy; Bennett, Coady, Boly, Doherty, Saïss (N'Diaye 68), Neves, Douglas (Costa 75), Cavaleiro, Bonatini, Jota. **Subs (unused)**: Norris, Batth, Price, Enobakhare, Vinagre. **Booked**: Douglas 65.
Sunderland 0	Ruiter; Love (Galloway 80), Browning, O'Shea, Wilson, Matthews, Gooch (Embleton 90+1), Cattermole, Gibson, Honeyman, Grabban (Vaughan 84). **Subs (unused)**: Steele, McGeady, Asoro, Beadling. **Booked**: Wilson 51, Honeyman 63, Browning 80. **Sent off**: Cattermole 62.

Attendance: 28,488	**Top Six**	**Pld**	**Pts**
	Wolves	21	48
	Cardiff City	20	43
	Bristol City	21	40
	Derby County	21	38
Referee:	Aston Villa	21	37
Jeremy Simpson	Sheffield United	21	37

Championship – December 15, 2017	
Sheffield Wed. 0	Wildsmith; Palmer, Loovens, van Aken, Fox, Jones, Butterfield (Lucas Joao 64), Hooper, Wallace, Reach, Rhodes (Nuhiu 64). **Subs (unused)**: Kean, Kean, Martias, Pudil, Abdi, Venancio. **Booked**: Butterfield 33. **Sent-off**: Fox 85.
Wolves 1 Neves 34	Ruddy; Bennett, Coady, Boly, Doherty, Saïss, Neves, Vinagre (Batth 67), Cavaleiro (N'Diaye 90+1), Bonatini (Costa 72), Jota. **Subs (unused)**: Norris, Gibbs-White, Miranda, Enobakhare. **Booked**: Jota 29, Bennett 43, Neves 82

Attendance: 23,809	**Top Six**	**Pld**	**Pts**
	Wolves	22	51
	Cardiff City	21	44
	Bristol City	21	40
	Derby County	21	38
Referee:	Aston Villa	21	37
Darren Bond	Sheffield United	21	37

Championship – December 23, 2017	
Wolves 1 Cavaleiro 40	Ruddy; Bennett, Coady, Boly, Doherty, Saiss, Neves, Douglas, Cavaleiro (Enobakhare 66), Bonatini (Costa 78), Jota (N'Diaye 88) **Subs (unused)**: Norris, Batth, Gibbs-White, Vinagre. **Booked**: Neves 72.
Ipswich Town 0	Bialkowski; Spence, Chambers, Webster, Kenlock, Connolly, Bru (Bishop 66), Ward, Waghorn (McGoldrick 72), Celina, Garner (Sears 78). **Subs (unused)**: Smith, Crowe, McDonnell, Webber. **Booked**: Waghorn 70, Connolly 80, Webster 86.

Attendance: 30,218	Top Six	Pld	Pts
	Wolves	23	54
	Cardiff City	23	47
	Derby County	23	44
	Bristol City	23	44
Referee: David Coote	Leeds United	23	39
	Aston Villa	23	38

Championship – December 26, 2017	
Millwall 2 Gregory 13 Cooper 72	Archer; McLaughlin (Romeo 52), Hutchinson, Cooper, Meredith, Wallace, Saville, Williams, O'Brien (Tunnicliffe 82), Elliott (Morison 60), Gregory. **Subs (unused):** Craig, Thompson, Onyedinma, Martin. **Booked:** Williams 20, McLaughlin 33, Hutchinson 90.
Wolves 2 Jota 45+4 Saïss 56	Ruddy; Bennett, Coady, Boly (Miranda 68), Doherty, Saïss, Neves, Douglas, Costa (N'Diaye 81), Jota, Cavaleiro (Bonatini HT). **Subs (unused)**: Norris, Batth, Enobakhare, Vinagre. **Booked:** Cavaleiro 7, Saïss 55, Coady 69.

Attendance: 13,121	Top Six	Pld	Pts
	Wolves	24	55
	Bristol City	24	47
	Cardiff City	24	47
	Derby County	24	45
Referee: Tim Robinson	Leeds United	24	42
	Sheffield United	24	41

Championship – December 30, 2017	
Bristol City 1 Reid 53	Fielding; Wright, Flint, Baker, Magnusson (Taylor 78), Brownhill (Eliasson 87), Pack, Smith, Bryan, Paterson (Steele 65), Reid. **Subs (unused)**: Woodrow, Kelly, Vyner, Leko. **Sent off**: Fielding 63.
Wolves 2 Douglas 66 Bennett 90+4	Ruddy; Batth, Coady, Boly, Doherty, Saïss, Neves, Douglas, Costa (Cavaleiro 62), Bonatini (Bennett 17), Jota (Enobakhare 88). **Subs (unused)**: Norris, N'Diaye, Gibbs-White, Hause. **Booked**: Neves 49. **Sent off**: Batth 14.

Attendance: 25,540	Top six:	Pld	Pts
	Wolves	25	58
	Derby County	25	48
	Bristol City	25	47
	Cardiff City	25	47
Referee: Peter Bankes	Leeds	25	42
	Sheffield United	25	41

Championship – January 2, 2018	
Wolves 3 Neves 57 Douglas 59 Jota 80	Ruddy; Bennett, Coady, Boly (Hause 83), Doherty, Saïss, Neves, Douglas, Costa (Cavaleiro 54), Bonatini, Jota (Enobakhare 81). **Subs (unused)**: Norris, N'Diaye, Gibbs-White, Vinagre. **Booked**: Neves 65, Boly 77.
Brentford 0	Bentley; Yennaris, Mepham, Bjelland, Barbet (Clarke 78), Woods, Mokotjo, Canos (Jozefzoon 64), Sawyers, Watkins, Vibe (Maupay 71). **Subs (unused)**: Daniels, MacLeod, McEachran, Marcondes. **Booked**: Watkins 22, Woods 56, Barbet 67.

Attendance: 28,475	Top Six	Pld	Pts
	Wolves	26	61
	Derby County	26	49
	Cardiff City	26	47
	Bristol City	26	47
Referee: Andy Madley	Aston Villa	26	44
	Leeds United	26	43

Championship – January 13, 2018	
Barnsley 0	Davies; Cavare, Pinnock, Lindsay, Yiadom, Gardner, Isgrove (Moncur HT), Mallan (Thiam 87), Potts, Hammill, Bradshaw (Moore 66). **Subs (unused)**: Townsend, McCarthy, Pearson, Brown. **Booked**: Mallan 43.
Wolves 0	Ruddy; Bennett, Coady, Boly, Doherty, Saïss, Neves (N'Diaye 90), Douglas, Costa (Cavaleiro 65), Bonatini (Mir Vicente 73), Jota. **Subs (unused)**: Norris, Gibbs-White, Enobakhare, Hause. **Booked**: Saïss 29, Jota 40.

Attendance: 16,050	Top Six	Pld	Pts
	Wolves	27	62
	Derby County	27	52
	Cardiff City	27	50
	Aston Villa	27	47
Referee:	Bristol City	27	47
Keith Stroud	Sheffield United	27	43

Championship – January 20, 2018	
Wolves 0	Ruddy; Bennett, Coady, Boly, Doherty (Costa HT), Saïss, Neves (Mir Vicente 78), Douglas (Gibbs-White HT), Cavaleiro, Bonatini, Jota. **Subs (unused):** N'Diaye, Batth, Miranda, Norris. **Booked:** Coady 38, Jota 65, Bennett 90.
Notts Forest 2 Dowell 40 Osborn 43	Smith; Lichaj, Worrall, Mancienne, Fox, Bouchalakis, Cash, Bridcutt (Clough 69), Osborn, Dowell (Darikwa 88), Brereton. **Subs (unused):** Henderson, Mills, Traore, Carayol, Vellios. **Booked:** Fox 6, Worrall 19, Bridcutt 30.

Attendance: 29,050	Top Six	Pld	Pts
	Wolves	28	62
	Derby County	28	53
	Cardiff City	28	51
	Aston Villa	28	50
Referee:	Bristol City	28	48
Robert Madley	Sheffield United	28	16

Championship – January 27, 2018			
Ipswich Town 0	Bialkowski; Spence, Carter-Vickers, Chambers, Knudsen, McGoldrick (Sears 83), Connolly, Gleeson (Hyam 84), Celina, Waghorn, Garner (Ward 84). **Subs (unused):** Webster, Crowe, Bru, Kenlock. **Booked:** Gleeson 24, Waghorn 12, Connolly 75.		
Wolves 1 Doherty 15	Ruddy; Bennett, Coady, Boly, Doherty, N'Diaye, Neves, Douglas, Costa (Enobakhare 78), Jota, Cavaleiro (Bonatini 72). **Subs (unused):** Norris, Batth, Gibbs-White, Miranda, Vinagre. **Booked:** N'Diaye 84.		
Attendance: 15,971	**Top Six**	**Pld**	**Pts**
	Wolves	29	65
	Derby County	28	53
	Cardiff City	28	51
	Bristol City	29	51
Referee:	Aston Villa	28	50
Simon Hooper	Fulham	29	48

Championship – February 3, 2018			
Wolves 3 Neves 5 Jota 30 Cavaleiro 76	Ruddy; Bennett, Coady, Boly, Doherty, N'Diaye, Neves, Douglas, Costa (Bonatini 65), Jota (Gibbs-White 81), Cavaleiro (Afobe 77). **Subs (unused)**: Norris, Batth, Enobakhare, Hause.		
Sheffield United 0	Moore; Basham (Leonard 71), Stearman, O'Connell, Baldock, Evans, Fleck, Stevens, Holmes (Donaldson 71), Wilson (Eastwood 76), Clarke. **Subs (unused):** Lundstram, Sharp, Duffy, Lafferty. **Sent off:** Moore 73.		
Attendance: 29,311	**Top Six**	**Pld**	**Pts**
	Wolves	30	68
	Derby County	30	57
	Aston Villa	30	56
	Cardiff City	29	54
Referee:	Fulham	30	51
Darren Bond	Bristol City	30	51

Championship – February 10, 2018	
Wolves 2 N'Diaye 12 Costa 21	Ruddy; Bennett, Coady, Boly, Doherty, N'Diaye, Neves, Douglas, Costa (Gibbs-White 77), Cavaleiro (Afobe 65), Jota. **Subs (unused):** Norris, Batth, Mir Vicente, Miranda, Vinagre.
QPR 1 Washington 51	Smithies; Perch (Eze 42), Onuoha, Lynch, Wszolek, Cousins (Smith HT), Robinson, Scowen, Bidwell, Freeman, Washington. Subs not used: Ingram, Baptiste, Chair, Osayi-Samuel, Obeh. **Booked:** Lynch 40, Cousins 45, Freeman 64.

Attendance: 30,168	**Top Six**	**Pld**	**Pts**
	Wolves	31	71
	Derby County	31	58
	Aston Villa	30	56
	Cardiff City	30	55
Referee:	Fulham	31	52
Geoff Eltringham	Bristol City	31	52

Willy Boly and QPR's Jack Robinson challenge for the ball during Wolves' 2-1 home victory.

Championship – February 17, 2018			
Preston NE 1 Browne 52	Rudd; Fisher, Huntington, Davies, Earl, Welsh, Johnson (Harrop 88); Bodin, Browne, Brakhuizen (Moult 88); Robinson (Horgan 70). **Subs (unused):** Maxwell, Woods, Spurr, O'Reilly. **Booked:** Fisher 31, Barkhuizen 59. **Sent off:** Welsh 59.		
Wolves 1 Costa 61	Ruddy; Bennett, Coady, Boly, Doherty, N'Diaye (Afobe 62), Neves, Douglas, Costa (Saiss 81), Cavaleiro (Bonatini 89), Jota. **Subs (unused):** Norris, Batth, Gibbs-White, Miranda.		
Attendance: 18,570	**Top Six**	**Pld**	**Pts**
	Wolves	32	71
	Cardiff City	32	61
	Aston Villa	32	59
	Derby County	32	58
Referee:	Fulham	32	55
Robert Jones	Bristol City	31	52

The pre-match team huddle in front of the loyal away supporters at Preston.

Championship – February 21, 2018	
Wolves 2 Lewis (og) 14 N'Diaye 25	Ruddy; Bennett, Coady, Boly, Doherty, N'Diaye (Gibbs-White 69), Neves, Douglas, Costa (Saïss HT), Jota, Cavaleiro (Afobe 60). **Subs (unused):** Norris, Batth, Miranda, Bonatini. **Booked:** Neves 36, N'Diaye 52, Jota 75.
Norwich City 2 Zimmermann 27 Oliveira 90+3	Gunn; Hanley, Zimmermann, Klose, Reid, Leitner, Vrancic (Hernandez 83), Lewis, Maddison, Watkins (Murphy 83), Srbeny (Oliveira 68). **Subs (unused):** McGovern, Husband, Raggett, Tettey.

Attendance:	Top Six	Pld	Pts
29,100	Wolves	33	73
	Cardiff City	33	64
	Aston Villa	33	60
	Derby County	33	59
Referee:	Fulham	33	56
James Linington	Bristol City	33	54

Championship – February 24, 2018	
Fulham 2 Sessegnon 38 Mitrovic 71	Bettinelli; Fredericks, Kalas, Ream, Targett, Cairney (Odoi 90+2), McDonald, Johansen, Ayite (Ojo 64), Mitrovic, Ryan, Sessegnon. **Subs (unused):** Button, Fonte, Norwood, Christie, Kamara. **Booked:** Targett 48
Wolves 0	Ruddy; Bennett, Coady, Boly, Doherty, Saïss (Afobe 77), N'Diaye (Gibbs-White 63), Douglas, Costa (Jota 63), Bonatini, Cavaleiro. **Subs (unused):** Norris, Batth, Miranda, Hause. **Booked:** Douglas 69, Boly 75.

Attendance:	Top Six	Pld	Pts
23,510	Wolves	34	73
	Cardiff City	33	64
	Aston Villa	34	63
	Derby County	34	60
Referee:	Fulham	34	59
Peter Bankes	Bristol City	33	54

Championship – March 7, 2018

Leeds United 0	Peacock-Farrell; Berardi, Jansson, Cooper (Pennington 36), Anita, Phillips, Forshaw, Dallas, Saiz, Sack (Hernandez HT), Lasogga (Ekuban 73). **Subs (unused):** Wiedwald, Alioski, O'Kane, Vieira. **Booked:** Forshaw 23, Hernandez 64.
Wolves 3 Saïss 28 Boly 45 Afobe 74	Ruddy; Batth, Coady, Boly, Doherty, N'Diaye, Saïss, Douglas, Cavaleiro (Gibbs-White 86), Bonatini (Afobe 70), Jota (Costa 75). **Subs (unused):** Norris, Bennett, Miranda, Hause.

Attendance:	Top Six	Pld	Pts
26,434	Wolves	35	76
	Cardiff City	35	70
	Aston Villa	35	66
	Fulham	36	65
Referee:	Derby County	36	61
Tim Robinson	Middlesbrough	36	58

Championship – March 10, 2018

Aston Villa 4 Adomah 8 Chester 57 Grabban 62 Bjarnason 85	Johnstone; El Mohamady, Chester, Terry, Taylor, Jedinak, Snodgrass, Grealish, Hourihane (Lansbury 81), Adomah (Bjarnason 75), Grabban (Hogan 86). **Subs (unused):** Bunn, Bree, Onomah, Davis. **Booked:** Adomah 44, Hourihane 79, Grealish 83
Wolves 1 Jota 20	Ruddy; Batth (Saïss 68), Coady, Boly, Doherty, N'Diaye, Neves, Douglas, Cavaleiro (Afobe 67), Bonatini, Jota (Costa 76). **Subs (unused):** Norris, Bennett, Miranda, Gibbs-White. **Booked:** Batth 37, Jota 39, N'Diaye 55, Coady 73, Costa 80.

Attendance:	Top Six	Pld	Pts
27,836	Wolves	36	76
	Cardiff City	36	73
	Aston Villa	36	69
	Fulham	37	68
Referee:	Derby County	36	61
David Coote	Middlesbrough	37	61

Championship – March 13, 2018	
Wolves 3 Doherty 40, 73 Afobe 58	Ruddy; Bennett, Coady, Boly, Doherty, Saïss (N'Diaye 78), Neves, Douglas, Costa, Afobe (Bonatini 72), Jota (Cavaleiro 25). **Subs (unused):** Norris, Batth, Gibbs-White, Miranda. **Booked:** Bennett 85.
Reading 0	Jaakkola; Gunter, Ilori, Moore, Blackett, Edwards, Evans (Bacuna 63), Clement, Aluko, Bodvarsson (Smith 83), Barrow. **Subs (unused):** Mannone, Kermorgant, Rinomhota, Loader, Holmes. **Booked:** Gunter 51, Evans 54.

Attendance:	Top Six	Pld	Pts
27,341	Wolves	37	79
	Cardiff City	37	76
	Aston Villa	37	69
	Fulham	37	68
Referee:	Derby County	37	62
Robert Jones	Middlesbrough	37	61

Championship – March 17, 2018	
Wolves 3 Costa 15 Afobe 41, 56	Ruddy; Bennett, Coady, Boly, Doherty, Saïss, Neves (N'Diaye 90+1), Douglas, Costa, Afobe (Bonatini 82), Cavaleiro (Gibbs-White 76). **Subs (unused):** Norris, Batth, Mir Vicente, Miranda.
Burton Albion 1 Dyer 44	Bywater; Flanagan, Naylor, Buxton, McFadzean (Varney 45), McCrory, Sordell (Sbarra HT), Davenport, Akpan, Dyer, Boyce (Egert 82). **Subs (unused):** Campbell, Murphy, Bent, Barker. **Booked:** Sbarra 53.

Attendance:	Top Six	Pld	Pts
29,977	Wolves	38	82
	Cardiff City	37	76
	Fulham	38	69
	Aston Villa	38	69
Referee:	Derby County	37	62
Geoff Eltringham	Middlesbrough	38	62

Championship – March 30, 2018	
Middlesbrough 1 Bamford 90+4	Randolph; Shotton (Cranie 70), Ayala, Gibson, Friend, Clayton (Assombalonga 70), Leadbitter (Howson 63), Besic, Traore. Bamford, Downing. **Subs (unused):** Konstantopoulos, Fry, Harrison, Baker. **Booked:** Leadbitter 11, Shotton 61, Cranie 90.
Wolves 2 Costa 32 Cavaleiro 37	Ruddy; Bennett, Coady, Boly, Doherty, Saïss, Neves, Douglas, Costa (Gibbs-White 84), Afobe (Bonatini 63), Cavaleiro (N'Diaye 58). **Subs (unused):** Norris, Batth, Vinagre, Hause. **Booked:** Ruddy 41, Saïss 66. **Sent off:** Neves 56, Doherty 71.

Attendance:	Top Six	Pld	Pts
27,658	Wolves	39	85
	Cardiff City	38	79
	Fulham	39	72
	Aston Villa	38	69
Referee:	Derby County	38	62
Stuart Attwell	Middlesbrough	39	62

Championship – April 3, 2018	
Wolves 2 Jota 18 (pen) Buur 83	Ruddy; Miranda (Afobe, HT), Coady, Boly, Bennett, N'Diaye (Gibbs-White 77), Saïss, Douglas, Costa, Cavaleiro, Jota (Buur 70). **Subs (unused):** Norris, Batth, Hause, Bonatini.
Hull City 2 Meyler 37 (pen) Bennett 78 (og)	McGregor; Tomori, Hector, MacDonald, Clark, Aina, Meyler, Henriksen, Kingsley (Campbell 70), Toral (Irvine 61), Dicko (Grosicki 65). **Subs (unused):** Mazuch, Marshall, Bowen, Stewart. **Booked:** Toral 9, Campbell 79, Tomori 87.

Attendance:	Top Six	Pld	Pts
29,718	Wolves	40	86
	Cardiff City	39	80
	Fulham	40	75
	Aston Villa	40	73
Referee:	Derby County	39	65
Darren England	Middlesbrough	40	63

Championship – April 6, 2018	
Cardiff City 0	Etheridge; Peltier, Morrison, Bamba, Bennett, Wildschut (Madine 71), Paterson (Mendez-Lang 51). Gunnarsson, Bryson, Zohore (Pilkington 84), Hoilett. **Subs (unused):** Ecuele Manga, Damour, Murphy, Traore. **Booked:** Peltier 62, Morrison 66
Wolves 1 Neves 67	Ruddy; Bennett, Coady, Boly, Doherty, Saïss, Neves, Douglas, Jota (Cavaleiro 67), Afobe (N'Diaye 78), Bonatini (Costa 58). **Subs (unused):** Norris, Batth, Gibbs-White, Hause.

Attendance:	Top six:	Pld	Pts
29,317	Wolves	41	89
	Cardiff	40	80
	Fulham	40	75
	Aston Villa	40	73
Referee:	Derby County	39	65
Mike Dean	Middlesbrough	40	63

Championship – April 11, 2018	
Wolves 2 Jota 6 Neves 51	Ruddy; Bennett, Coady, Boly, Doherty, Saïss, Neves, Douglas, Cavaleiro (Gibbs-White 82), Afobe (Costa 66), Jota (Bonatini 74). **Subs (unused):** Norris, N'Diaye, Batth, Hause. **Booked:** Bennett 61.
Derby County 0	Carson; Wisdom, Pearce, Davies, Baird, Huddlestone, Ledley (Palmer 73), Weimann, Vydra (Hanson 85), Lawrence, Nugent (Jerome 82). **Subs (unused):** Forsyth, Keogh, Roos, Thomas.

Attendance:	Top Six	Pld	Pts
28,503	Wolves	42	92
	Fulham	42	81
	Cardiff City	41	80
	Aston Villa	42	76
Referee:	Derby County	41	68
Tim Robinson	Millwall	42	68

Championship – April 15, 2018	
Wolves 2 Jota 21 Afobe 87	Ruddy; Bennett, Coady, Boly, Doherty, Saïss, Neves (N'Diaye 70), Douglas, Costa, Cavaleiro (Bonatini 16), Jota (Afobe 74). **Subs (unused):** Norris, Batth, Gibbs-White, Hause, Bonatini.
Birmingham City 0	Stockdale; Harding, Morrison, Dean, Grounds (Maghoma 62), Colin, Ndoye (Gardner 78), Kieftenbeld (Roberts 54), Jota, Davis, Jutkiewicz. **Subs (unused):** Lowe, Dacre-Cogley, Kuszczak, Lubala. **Booked:** Grounds 33, Morrison 43. **Sent off:** Dean 52.

Attendance: 29,536	**Top Six**	**Pld**	**Pts**
	Wolves	43	95
	Cardiff City	42	83
	Fulham	43	82
	Aston Villa	43	79
Referee:	Middlesbrough	43	69
Andy Davies	Millwall	43	69

Conor Coady leads the celebrations as promotion to the Premier League is confirmed with a 2-0 win over Birmingham.

Championship – April 21, 2018	
Bolton W. 0	Alnwick; Flanagan, Wheater, Beevers, Robinson, Pratley (Vela 58), Henry, Morais, Ameobi, Buckley (Noone 65), Le Fondre (Clough 79). **Subs (unused):** Andrew Taylor, Wilbraham, Burke, Howard. **Booked:** Wheater 56.
Wolves 4 Douglas 16 Afobe 45+1 Jota 53 Coady 66 (pen)	Ruddy; Batth, Coady, Boly, Doherty, Saïss (N'Diaye 81), Neves, Douglas, Costa, Afobe (Bonatini 68), Jota (Gibbs-White 68). **Subs (unused):** Norris, Bennett, Miranda, Hause. **Booked:** Batth 46.

Attendance:	Top Six	Pld	Pts
19,092	Wolves	44	98
	Cardiff City	43	86
	Fulham	44	85
	Aston Villa	44	82
Referee:	Middlesbrough	44	72
Keith Stroud	Millwall	44	69

A 4-0 away win, the Championship title is secured and it's time to party.

Championship – April 28, 2018	
Wolves 0	Ruddy; Batth, Coady, Boly, Doherty, Saïss, Neves, Douglas, Costa (Enobakhare 74), Afobe (Bonatini 55), Jota (Gibbs-White 87). **Subs (unused):** Norris, N'Diaye, Miranda, Hause. **Booked:** Saïss 83.
Sheffield Wednesday 0	Dawson; Venancio, Lees, Pudil, Reach, Pelupessy, Bannan, Thornley, Lucas Joao (Matias 60), Nuhiu, Forestieri **Subs (unused):** Jones, Rhodes, Boyd, Baker, Wildsmith, Nielsen.

Attendance: 29,794	Top six:	Pld	Pts
	Wolves	45	99
	Cardiff City	45	89
	Fulham	45	88
	Aston Villa	45	83
Referee:	Middlesbrough	45	75
Simon Hooper	Derby County	45	72

Championship – May 6, 2018	
Sunderland 3 Ejaria 19 Fletcher 45 McNair 66	Steele; Matthews, O'Shea (Mumba 87), Wilson, Oviedo (Hume 71), Robson, Asoro, McNair, (Embleton 75), Ejaria, Molyneux, Fletcher. **Subs (unused):** Camp, McManaman, Maja, Clarke-Salter.
Wolves 0	Norris (Burgoyne 71); Batth, Coady, Miranda, Doherty, Saïss, Neves, Douglas, Costa (Enobakhare 56), Gibbs-White (Bonatini 56), Jota. **Subs (unused):** Afobe, Vinagre, Hause, N'Diaye.

Attendance: 28,452	Top Six	Pld	Pts
	Wolves	46	99
	Cardiff City	46	90
	Fulham	46	88
	Aston Villa	46	83
Referee:	Middlesbrough	46	76
Jeremy Simpson	Derby County	46	75

Appendix 2 – League Cup

League Cup – August 8, 2017	
Wolves 1 Dicko 76	Norris; Bennett, Batth, Boly, Price, Graham, Edwards, (Enobakhare 69), Ronan (Saïss 81), Vinagre, Bonatini (Jota 69), Dicko. **Subs (unused):** Doherty, Burgoyne, Coady, Miranda.
Yeovil Town 0	Krysiak; Sowunmi, James, Nathan Smith, Alfei, Bailey,Connor Smith (Gray 81), Dickson, Browne, Zoko (Surridge 55), Khan (Olomola 66). **Subs (unused):** Maddison, Mugabi, Davies, Santos.
Attendance: 9,478	**Referee:** Robert Lewis

League Cup, Round 2 – August 22, 2017	
Southampton 0	Forster; Stephens, Bednarek (Redmond 72), Yoshida, Pied, Romeu, Ward-Prowse, McQueen, Tadic, Austin (Long 76), Boufal (Gabbiadini 76). **Subs (unused):** McCarthy, Soares, Davis, Bertrand. **Booked:** Austin 27, Romeu 45.
Wolves 2 Batth 67 Wilson 87	Norris; Bennett, Batth, Deslandes, Graham, Edwards, Price, Vinagre, Marshall (Ronan HT). Dicko (Zyro 74), Cavaleiro (Wilson 86). **Subs (unused):** Burgoyne, Goncalves, Johnson, Armstrong. **Booked:** Marshall 45, Zyro 75.
Attendance: 17,931	**Referee:** James Linington

League Cup, Round 3 – September 19, 2017	
Wolves 1 Enobakhare 98 (AET)	Norris; Batth, Coady, Miranda, Buur (Wilson 90), Price, N'Diaye, Deslandes (Douglas 60), Marshall (Ronan 68), Zyro (Cavaleiro 68), Enobakhare. **Subs (unused):** Burgoyne, Gibbs-White, Hause. **Booked:** Douglas 72, Batth 81, Price 101, N'Diaye 102.
Bristol Rovers 0	Slocombe; Leadbitter (Partington 97), Lockyer, Broadbent (Moore 105), Bola, O'Clarke, Lines, Sercombe, Bodin, Nichols (Telford 86), Harrison (Gaffney 90+3). **Subs (unused):** Smith, Brown, Sinclair. **Booked:** Harrison 58, Telford 90. **Sent off:** Lockyer 119.
Attendance: 12,740	**Referee:** Tony Harrington

Donovan Wilson is fouled by Bristol Rovers' Wales international Tom Lockyer, who was shown the red card for this challenge.

League Cup, Round 4 – October 24, 2017	
Manchester City 0	Bravo; Dainlo (Walker 103), Adarabioyo (Stones 90), Mangala, Zinchenko, Gundogan, Yaya Toure, Sterling, Bernardo Silva (Sane 95), Jesus (De Bruyne 82), Aguero. **Subs (unused):** Ederson, Delph, Nmecha. **Booked:** Toure 93.
Wolves 0	Norris; Batth, Coady, Hause, Bennett, Price, N'Diaye, Vinagre, Marshall (Ronan 79), Enobakhare (Bonatini 90), Costa (Cavaleiro 79). **Subs (unused):** Burgoyne, Doherty, Miranda, Deslandes. **Booked:** Price 82, Bennett 84.
Attendance: 50,755	**Referee:** Kevin Friend
Man City won 4-1 on penalties (after extra time) **Penalty Shoot-out:** 0-1 (Bonatini), 1-1 (De Bruyne), 2-1 (Toure), N'Diaye missed, Coady missed, 3-1 (Sane), 4-1 (Aguero).	

A dejected Conor Coady walks away after his miss in the penalty shoot-out.

Appendix 3 – FA Cup

FA Cup Round 3 – January 6, 2018	
Wolves 0	Norris; Bennett, Coady, Hause, Doherty, Gibbs-White (Douglas 45+1), N'Diaye, Vinagre, Costa, Bonatini (Mir Vicente 77), Enobakhare (Cavaleiro 65). **Subs (unused):** Burgoyne, Miranda, Goncalves, Buur. **Sent off:** Vinagre 40.
Swansea City 0	Nordfeldt; van der Hoorn, Fernandez (Jordan Ayew 56), Bartley, Roberts, Renato Sanches (Carroll 34), Fer, Olsson, Dyer, Bony (Mesa 74), Routledge. **Subs (unused):** Mulder, Narsingh, Fulton, McBurnie. **Booked:** Bartley 59, Dyer 69. Sent-off: Fer 67.
Attendance: 22,967	**Referee:** Anthony Taylor

FA Cup Round 3 replay – January 17, 2018	
Swansea City 2 Ayew 11 Bony 69	Nordfeldt; Naughton, Fernandez, Mawson, Roberts, Fer, Mesa (Ki Sung-yueng 73), Carroll, Narsingh (Dyer 73), Bony (Clucas 79), Jordan Ayew. **Subs (unused):** Mulder, Britton, Bartley, McBurnie. **Booked:** Fer.
Wolves 1 Jota 66	Norris; Batth, Miranda, Hause, Doherty, Gibbs-White, N'Diaye, Douglas, Costa (Saiss 73), Mir Vicente (Bonatini 64), Enobakhare (Jota 64). **Subs (unused):** Burgoyne, Bennett, Neves, Coady. **Booked:** N'Diaye 34, Douglas 72, Saïss 90.
Attendance: 8,294	**Referee:** Chris Kavanagh

Appendix 4 – Appearances & Goalscorers

Championship

Appearances: Coady 45, Doherty 45, Ruddy 45, Jota 43 (1), Neves 42, Douglas 38 (1), Saïss 37 (5), Boly 36, Cavaleiro 31 (12), Bonatini 29 (13), Bennett 27 (2), Costa 21 (15), Miranda 16 (1), Batth 15 (1), N'Diaye 13 (19), Vinagre 8 (1), Afobe 7 (9), Enobakhare 5 (17), Gibbs-White 1 (12), Marshall 1 (5), Norris 1, Dicko (5), Price (5), Ronan (3), Mir Vicente (2), Burgoyne (1) Buur (1), Deslandes (1), Edwards (1), Graham (1), Hause (1).

Goals: Jota 17, Bonatini 12, Cavaleiro 9, Afobe 6, Neves 6, Costa 5, Douglas 5, Doherty 4, Saïss 4, Boly 3, N'Diaye 3, Buur 1, Enobakhare 1, Bennett 1, Dicko 1, Batth 1, Coady 1, Vinagre 1, Own goal 1.

Léo Bonatini celebrates his goal against Birmingham.

Cup

Appearances: Norris 6, Batth 5, Enobakhare 4 (2), Bennett 4, N'Diaye 4, Price 4, Vinagre 4, Coady 3, Costa 3, Hause 3, Marshall 3, Bonatini 2 (2), Deslandes 2, Dicko 2, Doherty 2, Edwards 2, Gibbs-White 2, Graham 2, Miranda 2, Cavaleiro 1 (3),Ronan 1 (3), Douglas 1 (2), Mir Vicente 1 (1). Buur 1, Zyro 1 (1), Boly 1, Saïss (2), Jota (2), Wilson (1).

Goals: Batth 1, Dicko 1, Enobakhare 1, Jota 1, Wilson 1.

Jota scores in the FA Cup replay against Swansea City at the Liberty Stadium.

Benik Afobe scores Wolves' second goal against Birmingham in April.

Goals Timeline (minutes when goals were scored)

1-10: Jota (Burton A), Neves (Sheff Utd H), 6 Neves (Hull A). Jota (Derby H), 8 Bonatini (Birmingham A), 9 Saïss (Fulham H), 10 Jota (Millwall H).

11-20: 11 Saïss (Burton A), 12 N'Diaye (QPR H), 13 Boly (Bolton H), 14 Lewis own goal (Norwich H), 15 Douglas (Leeds H), Doherty (Ipswich A), Costa (Burton H), 16 Cavaleiro (Reading A), Douglas (Bolton A), 18 Boly (Norwich A), Jota pen (Hull H), 20 Jota (Villa A).

21-30: 21 Costa (QPR H), Jota (Birmingham H), 25 Bonatini (Bolton H), N'Diaye (Norwich H), 26 Bonatini (Fulham H), Cavaleiro (Leeds H), 28 Bonatini (Bristol City H), Saïss (Leeds A), 30 Jota (Sheff Utd H)

31-40: 32 Douglas (Derby A), Costa (Middlesbrough A), 33 Bonatini (Middlesbrough H), 34 Neves (Sheff Wed A), 37 Cavaleiro (Middlesbrough A), 40 Doherty (Reading H), Cavaleiro (Ipswich H).

41-50: 41 Vinagre (Burton A), Afobe (Burton H), 43 Jota (Hull A), Bonatini (QPR A), 44 Cavaleiro (Preston H), 45 Boly (Leeds A), 45+1 Afobe (Bolton A), 45+4 Jota (Millwall A), 47 Jota (Nottm Forest A).

Player of the Season Rúben Neves, with his daughter, thanks the Wolves fans for their support.

51-60: 51 Neves (Derby H), 53 Jota (Bolton A), 54 Jota (Bristol City H), 55 Jota (Villa H), 56 Saïss (Millwall A), Afobe (Burton H), 57 Neves (Brentford H), 58 Afobe (Reading H), 59 Bonatini pen (Preston H), Douglas (Brentford H).

61-70: 61 Costa (Preston A), 62 Bonatini (Burton A), Cavaleiro pen (Bolton H), 63 Bonatini (Preston H), 66 Douglas (Bristol City A), Coady pen (Bolton A), 67 Bonatini (Cardiff H), Neves (Cardiff A).

71-80: 71 Bonatini (Villa H), 72 Bonatini (Norwich A), Jota (Leeds H), 73 Doherty (Reading H), 74 Afobe (Leeds A), 76 Cavaleiro (Derby A), Costa pen (Leeds H), Cavaleiro (Sheff Utd H), 80 Enobakhare (Barnsley H), Jota (Brentford H)

81-90: 81 Jota (Nottm Forest A), 82 Cavaleiro pen (Bolton H), 83 Buur (Hull H), 85 Batth (Bristol City H, 87 Jota (Bolton H), Afobe (Birmingham H), 88 Doherty (Reading A), 90 Dicko (Hull A), 90+3 N'Diaye (Barnsley H), 90+4 Bennett (Bristol City A).

The players who've taken Wolves back to the Premier League, with style and panache.

Nuno, the architect of Wolves' renaissance, and his talented backroom staff.

St David's Press

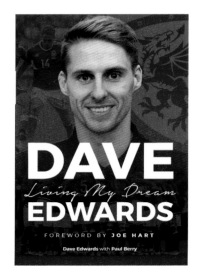

'A fascinating look at the journey made by all of us who set out as young kids with the dream of one day becoming a professional footballer.'
Joe Hart

'The life of a footballer is a very privileged one, and what comes through in this book is that Dave recognises that and never takes it for granted.'
Geoff Peters, TalkSport

'It is rare to get an insight into the dressing room from a footballer still playing the game. Dave's book provides a great understanding of the life of an international footballer at a major tournament.'
Johnny Phillips, SkySports

'A fantastic behind-the-scenes insight of what it was like in the Welsh camp at Euro 2016. A special time and a great read.'
Gareth Bale

'Great to re-live the memories of a tournament which none of us will ever forget.'
Chris Coleman

As a football-mad young boy growing up in rural Shropshire, Dave Edwards dreamt of playing the game professionally and perhaps, one day, of wearing the red shirt of his father's homeland - Wales.

978 1 902719 641 – £13.99 – 224pp – 32pp of illustrations/photographs